UNDERSTANDING
REVELATION

UNDERSTANDING REVELATION

An Investigation of the Key Interpretational and Chronological
Questions Which Surround the Book of Revelation

by

Gary G. Cohen

MOODY PRESS

CHICAGO

Library of Congress Cataloging in Publication Data

Cohen, Gary G.
    Understanding Revelation.
    Revision of the author's thesis, Grace Seminary.
    Bibliography: p. 182.
    1. Bible. N.T. Revelation—Prophecies. I. Title.
BS2825.2.C56 1978   228'.07   77-18065
ISBN 0-8024-9022-0

The American Standard Version of 1901 will be used for all Scripture quotations unless otherwise noted.[1] The 23rd edition of the Nestle Greek text of the New Testament is the foundational basis for this study, and will be referred to as necessary.[2]

[1]*The Holy Bible.* American Standard Version. (New York: Nelson, 1901).
[2]Eberhard Nestle, Erwin Nestle, and Kurt Aland, *Novum Testamentum Graece. 23rd ed.* (Stuttgart: Privileg. Wurtt., 1957).

MOODY PRESS EDITION, 1978
Second Printing, 1978

Printed in the United States of America

To
the students of
Graham Bible College,
Bristol, Tennessee
and to
Steven Reed Cohen

Contents

CHAPTER   PAGE

List of Tables   9

Preface   11

Introduction   13

    Authorship and Date   19

1. Revelation 1: Basic Chronological Orientation   21

    Six Basic Approaches   23

        Critical   23

        Allegorical   24

        Preterit   24

        Historical   27

        Topical   32

        Futuristic   36

2. Revelation 2-3: The Chronological Problem of the Seven Churches   50

3. Revelation 4-5: The Chronological Problem of the Throne Scene   72

4. Revelation 6-19: Are the Seals, Trumpets, and Bowls Contemporaneous or Successive?   83

    Part A. Introductory Observations   83

    Part B. Succession within Each Series   86

    Part C. Are the Seals, Trumpets, and Bowls Successive?   94

    Part D. Objections to the Succession View   108

    Part E. Conclusion   123

5.   Revelation 6-19: The Chronological Placing
     of the Insets   127
     The 144,000 sealed (Rev 7:1-8)   128
     The great multitude (Rev 7:9-17)   130
     The angel and the little book (Rev 10:1-11)   132
     The two witnesses (Rev 11:1-13)   132
     The woman and the Dragon (Rev 12)   136
     The Beast (Rev 13)   141
     The 144,000 upon Zion (Rev 14:1-5)   144
     The harvest (Rev 14:14-20)   147
     The destruction of Babylon (Rev 17-18)   149
     The marriage of the Lamb (Rev 19:1-10)   156
     The revelation of Christ (Rev 19:11-21)   160

6.   Revelation 20-22: The Chronology of the
     Millennium and the Eternal State   164

    Conclusion   178
    Selected bibliography   182

List of Tables

NUMBER   PAGE

1. Albert Barnes's Historical Interpretation
    of Revelation 6-19   28

2. The Seven Year Tribulation Period in the
    Scriptures   38

3. A Comparison Between Daniel's Fourth
    Beast and the Beast of the Revelation   45

4. A Comparison Between the Chronology of
    the Seven Year Tribulation Period and
    Five Chronological Specifications from
    the Apocalypse   46

5. Reasons for Accepting the Futuristic
    Approach   49

6. Philip Schaff's Outline of the Periods of
    Church History   57

7. The Chronological Pattern of the
    Unloosing of the Judgments   98

8. Thunders, Voices, Lightnings, Earthquakes,
    and Hail as Found in Revelation 4-19   122

9. The Chronology of the Tribulation   162

Preface

It is here proper to confess that this present work is built upon the labors of those many Christian gentlemen of yesterday and today who have given themselves over to endless hours of prayerful and scholarly study of the book of Revelation. Where I have at times been forced to vary from the opinions of some of the great names in biblical scholarship, it is trusted that the reader will understand that the general overall ability and accuracy of these scholars of proven devotion and worth has in no way been challenged.

The draft of this book was originally prepared as a doctoral dissertation at Grace Theological Seminary, Winona Lake, Indiana. Deep gratitude is expressed to the faculty for its outstanding guidance and assistance.

A special word of appreciation must be given to my wife, Marion, for her constant assistance, and to Sharon and Caralee for their devotion. Finally, to the Lord Jesus Christ, the Revealer of the Apocalypse, the blessed Saviour, I offer my prayerful thanks for permitting me the privilege of engaging in this study of the "things which must shortly come to pass" (Rev 1:1).

It is my prayer that the Lord of the church will use these pages to promote a fuller understanding of His prophetic Word. Some topics here treated are quite difficult; nevertheless, I have suggested the answers that in my limited sight seem best to fit the evidence.

In any case, I hope that no reader, because of doubts concerning this or that detail, will fall into the error of missing the clear and wonderful message of biblical prophecy of God's constant control of the world, His plain promises to raise the dead and bring all those who believe on Christ into the joy of the eternal blessedness, His eventual doing away with all evil and evildoers, and Christ's soon coming and establishing His Kingdom, where He will be King of kings and reign in righteousness.

Introduction

The book of Revelation is one of God's great gifts to His church.[1] It reveals "things which must shortly come to pass" (Rev 1:1), and since these things are the ultimate triumph of Christ and the eternal glorification of the saints, this book has been a source of great comfort and encouragement to God's people ever since it was written, through the inspiration of the Holy Ghost, by the apostle John at c. A.D. 96.[2] Even though many Christians have not understood all the things in this book, they have always clearly seen that a safe harbor awaits every servant of Christ at journey's end. The Apocalypse reveals not only the awful struggle within the universe, but also the glorious consummation of all things. God will yet destroy Satan and his forces and dwell in New Jerusalem in communion with the redeemed for all eternity.

THE PROBLEM

This publication is devoted to a study of the problem of the chronology of the book of Revelation. Much confusion has existed on this topic down through the centuries, and this has consequently diminished for many the blessing which the book has to offer. This confusion has even caused some to abandon the hope of ever really understanding the Apocalypse. The difficulty stems from an inability even for many otherwise sound interpreters to come to definite and proper conclusions regarding the following three questions:

(1) *What is the relative chronological order of the major events of the book?* For example, are the seven seals, seven trumpets, and seven bowls of Revelation 6-16 three series of judgments that occur simultaneously or successively?

---

[1]The exact title of the book is expressed in the opening words of its first verse as found in the Greek New Testament, "A Revelation of Jesus Christ." The term *apocalypse* is a transliteration for the Greek word *revelation* and is likewise one of the acceptable titles of the work.
[2]Covered later in this book.

(2) *In what time periods, or dispensations, are the major events to be placed?* Do the judgments of the seals, trumpets, and bowls take place in a yet future seven year Tribulation period as some teach, or do they, as others aver, run their course over the entire church age, which has already spanned almost two thousand years? If a person is not sure, for example, whether the bowls of God's wrath (Rev 16) are now being poured on to the earth or are yet stored up for a future period of tribulation, then how can he hope to interpret the individual verses of chapter 16? If he holds an incorrect view, his misunderstanding is so much the greater.

Is the 1000 year reign of Christ, spoken of in Revelation 20, taking place now, or is it yet to come? As the answer to this question affects one's entire system of eschatology as well as one's entire hermeneutical approach to the Old Testament prophecies of the Kingdom, its gravity can hardly be overestimated.

(3) *Are the time designations to be taken literally?* Revelation 9:5, 10 speak of "five months," Revelation 11:2 and 13:5 mention "forty and two months," Revelation 11:3 and 12:6 deal with "a thousand two hundred and three-score days," Revelation 11:9, 11 is concerned with "three days and an half," and Revelation 20:2-3, 5, 7 declares Satan to be bound for "a thousand years." If all or most of these are literal periods then a wide avenue of aid is opened towards the understanding of the book. If all or most of these are figures of speech so that the "forty and two months" of Revelation 13:5 may represent 1,260 years according to one,[3] or the present "gospel age" of almost two thousand years according to another,[4] then each interpreter must intrepidly tread the road of unending suggestions as to the meaning of these numbers, and then finally advance his own opinions with reservations.

Until the above major questions are settled, and settled correctly, the book of Revelation cannot but to a large measure either (1) remain a mystery, or (2) be misinterpreted. To the solution of these questions this treatise is primarily devoted. It will attempt to solve these and other issues so that the major events spoken of in the book of Revelation can be placed in their proper dispensational time period, and in their correct chronological order of

[3]Albert Barnes, *Revelation* (Grand Rapids: Baker, 1949), pp. 323-24.
[4]W. Hendriksen, *More Than Conquerors* (Grand Rapids: Baker, 1960), p. 174.

succession, which event happens first, second, third, until the final event occurs.

Once this task, surrounded by so much controversy, is accomplished, a framework will exist upon which the interpreter can rightly position and interpret each and every verse of the Apocalypse. The purpose of this publication is to establish this true chronological framework, and the immensity of this one undertaking places the orientation of every single verse, the answering of every problem, and the airing of the views held on each question down through the centuries of church history beyond the scope of this study. As however the various issues pertaining to the chronology of the Apocalypse are taken up, the major exponents of the various views will be noted and all pertinent arguments shall be treated.

PRESUPPOSITIONS

This book is written from the conservative standpoint, believing that the Apocalypse in its original Greek autographs is a canonical portion of the inerrant, inspired, written Word of God. The grammatico-historico-theological method of hermeneutics is used. This method interprets words and numbers literally unless their context gives warrant for taking them in a figurative or symbolical sense. It recognizes figures of speech, but insists that every figure has an intended real significance which can and must be ascertained according to the rules of common sense and evidence. Thus the wild beast of Revelation 13 with seven heads and ten horns is seen to be a symbolical figure, but when Scripture is compared to Scripture and the evidence weighed, this figure must be seen to represent a real entity—be it a person, a world power, or a world power personified in its dictator. As Ironside has said,

> This book is a book of symbols. But the careful student of the Word need not exercise his own ingenuity in order to think out the meaning of the symbols. It may be laid down as a principle of first importance that every symbol used in Revelation is explained or alluded to somewhere else in the Bible.[5]

It is also recognized that the book of Revelation, like all Scripture, describes things in the language of appearance rather than in

[5] Harry A. Ironside, *Lectures on the Book of Revelation* (New York: Loizeaux, 1919), p. 13.

15

technical twentieth century terminology. It is written for the common man rather than for the professional philosopher and scientist. Yet, it does not contain error. Thus, in 6:13, when the account describes stars falling, the stars (*asteres*) cannot be limited to our modern definition of such, but may include everthing and anything which appears to one's sight like a star. Thus falling stars, once it is concluded that this is not a figure for falling angelic beings, could conceivably include any or all of the following: actual stars, immense, far away masses of burning gases; meteor showers; man-made satellites which to the unaided eye look like stars even though they give off light by reflection; and any other phenomenal, natural, supernatural, or man-made, which have this same star-like appearance.

The principle that Scripture is its own best interpreter is also here taken to be true on the ground that the entire Bible is an inspired unity. Thus just as light is made to come from many points above a surgical table to prevent shadows, so other portions of God's Word illuminate some of the dark spots in the Apocalypse. For this reason, eschatological Old Testament prophecies, especially those of the book of Daniel, and New Testament prophecies, chiefly the Olivet Discourse,[6] will be constantly integrated into this study.[7]

In addition to the usage of the above hermeneutical system, this examination will also be undertaken starting with certain eschatological beliefs. These are:

(1) The premillennial viewpoint is correct; Christ will come literally and personally with power and great glory to establish His thousand year earthly Kingdom (Isa 2:2-4; Dan 2:44; 7:13-14; Matt 25:31-46).

2) There is to be a future Tribulation period of seven years, which makes up the seventieth week of Daniel.[8] During this period, God will again deal with Israel as a nation, the man called

[6] Matt 24-25; Mark 13; and Luke 21 contain the Olivet Discourse.

[7] See the author's discussion of thirteen hermeneutical principles in "Hermeneutical Principles and Creation Theories." *Grace Journal*, vol. 5, no. 3 (fall 1964), pp. 18-23. Although in a different context, the principles and discussion apply here.

[8] The terms *Tribulation* or *Tribulation period* are to be understood to refer to the entire span of seven years encompassed within Daniel's seventieth week (Dan 9:27). The expression "the *Great Tribulation*" is however, reserved for the second half of this period (Matt 24:21). During this latter half of the period the Antichrist shall unleash a fearful persecution upon Israel and thus it is one of "Great Tribulation" (Matt 24:15-29, esp. v. 21; Dan 7:25).

For an excellent argument showing that Daniel's prophecy of Seventy weeks

the Antichrist will play the dominant role, and Israel will experience an unparalleled persecution (Jer 30:4-7; Dan 7:7-8, 15-28; 8:23-25; 9:20-27; Matt 24:3-31; John 5:23; 2 Thess 2:1-12).

3) The pretribulational viewpoint as to the Rapture is correct; Christ will come *for His church* at the Rapture before the beginning of the Tribulation (1 Thess 4:13-18), and again *with His church* at His "Revelation" at the end of the Tribulation period in order to crush His enemies and commence the millennial reign (Rev 19:11—20:6).

4) From the two declarations immediately above it is seen that there is a distinction in the program of God between the church in our present age and the nation Israel. The church will be raptured immediately before the Tribulation (3 above) but national Israel remains upon the earth to go through a fiery persecution until Jehovah rescues her (2 above). Thus there is every reason that the 144,000 sealed out of the tribes of the children of Israel in Revelation 7 should be taken as physically as well as spiritually true Jews.

This examination, built upon the works and findings of others, begins with the conviction that premillennialism is true, and that Daniel's seventieth week refers to a future seven year tribulation period, then starting from here it attempts to make manifest the chronology of the book of Revelation.

Should anyone read this work who has reservations with one or more of these assumptions, let it be said that each argument ought nevertheless to be examined on its own merits. Most of the proofs and conclusions do not depend on the assumptions made above for their validity, and others by their compelling nature and harmony tend to confirm the truth of the presupposition which undergirds them.

THE APOCALYPSE CAN BE UNDERSTOOD

At this point, in order to justify the present inquiry, it must be noted that a true knowledge of the book, which involves its basic chronological framework, is possible despite the fact that numerous and divergent interpretations are in circulation. Revelation 1:1, 3 declares,

---

deals with seventy weeks of "years" rather than with weeks of "days" see John C. Whitcomb, Jr. "Daniel's Great Seventy-Week Prophecy: An Exegetical Insight," pp. 1-4.

> The Revelation of Jesus Christ, which God gave him to show unto his servants, even the things which must shortly come to pass: and he sent and signified it by his angel unto his servant John .... Blessed is he that readeth, and they that hear the words of the prophecy, and keep the things which are written therein: for the time is at hand.

The very word *revelation* (*apokalupsis*) of Revelation 1:1 signifies a "disclosure" of something previously unknown, hidden, or beclouded.[9] Hence the meaning of the word itself argues that this "Revelation of Jesus Christ" is a means of *uncovering* (this is the etymological root of the word) the future, "things which must shortly come to pass." Also, verse 3 tells how blessed is the person who reads, hears, and keeps the things in this book. The inference can be unmistakably drawn that there is profit in reading and hearing the book because it is capable of being understood.

If the book was understood to a great extent when it was first written, it is more so today. Less than a century ago many great expositors thought that the Kingdom and peace would be brought in and the world converted before the second coming of Christ. They were postmillennialists.[10] Now with two world wars past, world communism, lawlessness, immorality, and unbelief everywhere on the increase, it is a rare person who yet thinks the postmillennial scheme to be a possibility. Thus the unfolding of history has eliminated this faulty system of interpreting portions of the Apocalypse.

The problem of understanding this book, with its great use of symbols rooted in the eschatological prophecies of the Old Testament, has been compared to the problem of understanding the parables of the Lord.[11] When the disciples asked Christ why He spoke in parables He explained His purpose in doing so, "that His disciples might understand but that those 'without' might be kept in ignorance respecting the future program of God" (Matt 13:10-15).[12] In like manner the Apocalypse can be an open book to believers, especially as the day of Christ's coming approaches, but to the unbelieving it is sealed shut.

---

[9]William F. Arndt and F. Wilbur Gingrich, *A Greek-English Lexicon of the New Testament and Other Early Christian Literature*, pp. 91-92.
[10]E.g., Charles Hodge, *Systematic Theology* 3: 861-66.
[11]Jacob B. Smith, *A Revelation of Jesus Christ*, p. 20.
[12]Ibid.

It seems fitting, before launching into the body of this work, to say a brief word concerning the authorship and date of the Apocalypse. That it was written by the apostle John (Rev 1:1,4,9) at about A.D. 95-96 is firmly substantiated by the testimony of Irenaeus (c. A.D. 170). Irenaeus was the pupil of Polycarp, who, in turn, sat at the feet of John himself, and thus his words in this area are of the first magnitude in importance and cannot easily be set aside.

> Irenaus says, "John also, the Lord's disciple, ... says in the Apocalypse," and then quotes 1:12-16; 5:6; 19:11-17 almost verbally, in *Against Heresies* (IV. xx. 11). In the same work (V. xxvi. 1) he does the same for 17:12-14. Indeed, he quotes from nearly every chapter in the book. In the same work (V. xxx. 3) he says that John saw the Apocalypse "towards the end of Domitian's reign" (A.D. 81-96).[13]

The tradition of the church fathers uniformly confirms Irenaeus' words. Those who advocate a later date, A.D. 100 or later (Harnack, et. al.), do so out of a biased attempt to apply the modern critical documentary hypothesis to every biblical writing. The advocates of an earlier date, A.D. 68-70 (F.W. Farrar, Schaff, et. al.), do so claiming that the internal evidence better seems to fit Nero's time, which assertion is both highly subjective and questionable.[14] Farrar declares that the writing must have taken place before the destruction of Jerusalem in A.D. 70 because Revelation 11:1-2 speaks of John measuring the Temple.[15] When one considers, however, the fact that events which have not yet occurred are prophesied to take place in the Temple (2 Thess 2:4), it can only be concluded that the Temple is again to be rebuilt. In light of this, one cannot be so dogmatic as Farrar in asserting that the Temple of Revelation 11:1-2 was the one torn down in A.D. 70. Besides, since John saw the Revelation at Patmos (Rev 1:9) it is manifestly clear that he did not physically measure the actual literal Temple at Jerusalem, but while in the spirit (Rev 1:10) measured a visionary Jerusalem Temple—be it one with physical properties or not (cf. Ezek 40-43).

---

[13]Henry C. Thiessen, *Introduction to the New Testament*, p. 317.
[14]Philip Schaff, *History of the Christian Church*, 1:426-29.
[15]F.W. Farrar, *The Early Days of Christianity*, p. 412.

Thus in the light of the uniform testimony of the church Fathers,[16] especially Irenaeus, it can be safely said that John the Apostle wrote Revelation at c. A.D. 95-96.[17] Alford,[18] Thiessen,[19] Lenski,[20] Barnes,[21] W. Milligan, Orr, Moffatt, Zahn, Hoyt,[22] and many others hold this view.

---

[16] Schaff, 1:427.

[17] For an exhaustive study of the authorship, date, and canonicity of the book of Revelation which advocates the views given above, see Henry Alford, The Greek Testament, vol. 4, Hebrews-Revelation, pp. 198-236.

[18] Ibid.

[19] Thiessen, pp. 321-23.

[20] R.C.H. Lenski, The Interpretation of St. John's Revelation, pp. 5-7.

[21] Barnes, pp. xlvi-xlix.

[22] Herman A. Hoyt, "Apocalypse" mimeographed syllabus, pp. 2-3.

1
Revelation 1: Basic Chronological Orientation

In this chapter several key items will be considered that relate not only to Revelation chapter 1, but also to one's basic understanding of the chronological framework of the book.

THE THREE DIVISIONS OF REVELATION 1:19

Write therefore the things which you saw, and the things which are, and the things which are about to come to pass after these things (Rev 1:19).[1]

This verse provides the reader with the inspired threefold division of the Apocalypse. First, the things which John had already seen, the vision of the risen Christ in chapter 1; second, the things "which are," namely the letters to seven of the Christian churches then existing in Asia, chapters 2-3; and third, the things "about to come to pass" yet in the future, the contents of chapters 4-22.[2]

The first division, "the things which you saw," consists of the vision of Christ in Revelation 1:10-20, following John's prologue

[1]Author's translation.

[2]It has been argued by Henry Alford, *The Greek Testament*, vol. 4, *Hebrews-Revelation*, p. 559, that the words of this verse could also be translated, "Write therefore the things which you have seen even what they mean, and the things which are about to happen after these things." This latter rendering would substitute a twofold division, consisting of (1) past things and their interpretations and (2) future things, for the threefold past, present, and future division denoted by the author's translation given above as well as by the translations of the King James

in the opening nine verses, which the apostle had already seen by the time he heard these words of Revelation 1:19. In this vision, the Saviour is walking in the midst of the seven churches that were represented by the seven lampstands (Rev 1:11-13, 20). Visual manifestation of His divine attributes was seen by John; flaming eyes showed the Lord's omniscience and feet like fine brass signified His power and readiness to judge.

In assigning this first section of the book its chronological place it must be noted that the words of Revelation 1:19, "Write . . . the things which you saw," do not relegate the vision of Christ walking among the churches to a time solely in the past. It only declares that this portion of the vision has already been seen.[3] In fact this porton of the Apocalypse contains a visual picture of the fulfillment of Christ's promise to His church when in giving the Great Commission He said, "All power is given unto me in heaven and in earth. . . . lo, I am with you always, even unto the end of the world" (Matt 28:18-20). Thus, chronologically speaking, it is safe to say, and all commentators do say, that Christ continues to walk

Version and the American Standard Version.

Lenski succinctly states the argument given in favor of the suggestion that *Kai ha eisin*, "and the-things-which-are," be translated, "even what they-mean," and then he rightly gives its refutation. He writes, "Nor can we understand *ha eisi* as 'what they mean' (i. e., what the things John saw *mean*). This is advocated because *eisi* is plural while *mellei* is singular, and because two more *eisi* follow in v. 20, all three are then to be understood as 'mean': the seven stars *mean* angels of the seven churches, the pedestal lamps *mean* seven churches. But this view is refuted by the temporal clause, 'the things about to occur *after these*,' i.e., after the ones that are. 'After these' cannot be referred back to mean, 'after the things thou didst see.' 'After these' joins 'are' and 'about to occur.' The present things and the future things are connected"(R.C.H. Lenski, *The Interpretation of St. John's Revelation*, pp. 78-79).

In agreement with Lenski on this point, it is also to be noted that the literal translation, "things which . . . and the things which . . . and the things which," certainly present to the reader an initial impression of a tripartite series. Further, since here the simple literal translation of *ha eisin*, "the things which are," yields the age old, yet sublime, division of past, present, and future, it cannot be permitted to yield to a more awkward and unusual translation which would see John here only given an explicit commission to write the past and future when the two chapters next to be written following this verse, chapters 2 and 3, plainly primarily deal with things then present, the seven churches of Asia.

The weight of the evidence clearly warrants the following of the simple literal translation, "the things which are," just as the KJV and ASV both have done. With this in mind the significance of the divisions of this verse can now be observed.

[3] The verb in the expression, "things which you saw" (Rev 1:19) is *eides*. It is in the aorist tense which signifies here that the seeing occurred and was completed in the past.

in the midst of His churches as their Lord, strength, and judge as long as they shall exist.[4]

The second division comprehends "the things which are" and consists of the messages to the seven churches which existed at the very time John was seeing and recording the visions of the Apocalypse. These messages are recorded in Revelation 2-3.

The third and final division concerns the "things which are about to come to pass after these things," and it narrates those events which will take place "after these things" (meta tauta), after the things pertaining to the seven churches. This last section of the book consists of Revelation 4:22 to 22:21.

While there is general agreement to the above threefold scheme of dividing the book, the problem, however, is that interpreters differ as to whether or not in actual historical events the "church history" of Revelation 2-3 ends with chapters 2-3 or whether it continues on into the "after these things" of Revelation 4-22. This question is the subject which will now be treated.

SIX BASIC APPROACHES

When the student seeks to discover the point in God's dealings with man on earth when the events of Revelation 4-22 begin, he finds that the answer to this question is determined by the basic approach that the various expositors take. There are six major outlooks which travel under diverse labels and often overlap: critical, allegorical, preterit, historical, topical, and futuristic.

CRITICAL

The critical approach denies either the inspiration or canonicity of the book of Revelation and sees the writing as a purely human composition based on the historical situation at the end of the first century A.D.[5] The Apocalypse is seen only to have utilized Jewish apocalyptical imagery in a fanciful style. Various historical and

---

[4]It is the lamentable truth that when expressions are used in connection with the book of Revelation such as "all commentators do say" or "there is general agreement," a qualification is always intended. So many writers with diverse and strange views exist that these expressions of uniform thought are only intended to encompass those expositors who are both orthodox and sober.

[5]See R.H. Charles, *A Critical and Exegetical Commentary on the Revelation of St. John, the International Critical Commentary*, vols. 1-2.

predictive errors are alleged by the critics. This view must be rejected completely by all who hold unreservedly to the inspiration and canonicity of Revelation.

ALLEGORICAL

The allegorical approach to the book denies the literal reality behind the descriptions of the narrated events, and takes the accounts to be solely allegories, parables, and metaphors which contain messages of spiritual encouragement. This view is contradicted by the first verse of the Revelation which states its purpose: "A Revelation of Jesus Christ, which God gave to Him, in order to show to His servants the things which are necessary shortly to come to pass."[6]

In Revelation 1:1, the Greek aorist (the Greek aorist tense denotes and emphasizes the accomplishment of an action or event) infinitive *deixai*, "to show," is used to express the purpose of the Revelation. This purpose is not here stated as one of encouragement, although this is undoubtedly one of the great intentions of the book, but the purpose enunciated is "to show . . . the things which are necessary shortly to come to pass." Thus the book, like the apocalyptical sections of Daniel and Zechariah, is designed to foretell future events and cannot be relegated into a class which merely encourages but does not in reality predict the future.

Those who adhere to this allegorical view generally either (1) hold the antisupernatural presupposition that prophecy is an *a priori* impossibility, and therefore this book does not predict the future in detail, but rather in a general and mystical way; or (2) they look upon the book as an insoluble mystery, and despairing of learning the future from it, turn to the mediating view that it is simply a pious fiction telling of the triumph of good over evil; or (3) they are despisers of the "surface" sense and seekers of the "hidden" meanings of Scripture. Believers who hold to the grammatico-historical method of hermeneutics can only reject this approach wholeheartedly.

PRETERIT

The preterit ("past") approach, first advanced in modern times by the Jesuit Alcazar in 1614,[7] looks upon the content of the book

[6]Author's translation.
[7]Lenski, p. 215.

as factual, but believes that everything in it, except for the visions of the eternal state in Revelation 21-22 and perhaps chapter 20, was already fulfilled at the time of John's writing.

F.W. Farrar, who advances this view, says that,

> The Apocalypse is what it professes to be—an inspired outline of contemporary history, and of the events to which the sixth decade of the first century gave immediate rise.[8]

To his mind, the second division of the book according to Revelation 1:19, "the things which are" refers to the historical scene A.D. 64-68 and embraces the preponderance of the account.[9] The third division, "the things which are about to come to pass after these things," Farrar takes to encompass the events in the Roman-Palestinian world of A.D. 68-70 such as the burning of the Temple of the Capitoline Jupiter and the fall of Jerusalem.[10] In this way he assigns Revelation 2-19 entirely to the vicinity of the tumultuous times from the beginning of the Neronian persecution in A.D. 64 to the ascension of Vespasian and the fall of Jerusalem in A.D. 70.[11] However, he sees the Beast, Nero, come alive again in Domitian (A.D. 81-96! Rev 13:3,14). Farrar argues that the book must deal primarily with events contemporary to John and those which occur *immediately* after on the ground that in Revelation 2:5, 16; 3:2; 11:14; 22:20 the word "speedily" (en *tachei*) is used and this cannot refer to any protracted period of centuries. To buttress this assertion he cites the fall of Jerusalem in A.D. 70 to be a "Second Advent" and "the second advent contemplated in many of the New Testament prophecies."[12]

Concerning these representative assertions made by certainly one of the most learned and able of the preterit school, several things may be noted. First, the repeated usage of the word "quickly" (en *tachei*) in the Apocalypse does not prove that all things which are so promised such as the Lord's second coming must occur within a limit of two or three years as Farrar demands.

[8]F.W. Farrar, *The Early Days of Christianity*, p. 429. As has been alluded to in the Introduction, Farrar believed the Revelation to have been written in the summer of A.D. 68 and his scheme of interpretation pivots on this assertion, pp. 412-13.

[9]Ibid., pp. 428-86, especially 428-34, 484-85.

[10]Ibid., pp. 432-33, 484-85.

[11]Ibid.

[12]Ibid., pp. 429, 432-33, 489.

Just such an accusing exaction is answered by 2 Peter 3:8-9 when it says,

> But forget not this one thing, beloved, that one day is with the Lord as a thousand years, and a thousand years as one day. The Lord is not slack concerning his promise, as some count slackness; but is long suffering to you-ward, not wishing that any should perish, but that all should come to repentance.

Second, such statements as, "the fall of Jerusalem was, in the fullest sense, the Second Advent of the Son of Man," show to what extremes the preterit theory may take even the most able expositor. If the events relating to the Beast and the False Prophet of Revelation 13 are assigned to Nero and Vespasian, such as Farrar assigns them,[13] then the logical outcome makes the coming of Christ on the white horse with His armies in Revelation 19 to occur in the lifetime of these men since at the time Christ casts both of these fiends alive into the lake of fire (Rev 19:20). How the fall of Jerusalem can be thought to fit the description of Revelation 19 is a wonder. How it can be put forth as that which John prayed for in Revelation 22:20 is more than a marvel.[14] Only by here using the false allegorizing or so-called spiritual method of interpretation can such an exegesis be brought forward; and Farrar, as preterit champion, is not unfriendly to this school when expounding the Revelation.[15]

Third, the preterit, like the allegorical approach, comes into conflict with the avowed purpose of the Revelation as it is expressed in Revelation 1:1: "A Revelation of Jesus Christ, which God gave to Him *in order to show to* His servants *the things which are necessary shortly to come to pass.*"[16] If the date of John's writing this work is in fact c. A.D. 95-96 as has been advocated as almost a certainty in the Introduction, then how can this purpose be accomplished according to the preterit view, which places its exposition of Revelation 2-19 and possibly 20 into the bounds of the years A.D. 64-70 or 64-96? Even if the early date advocated by Farrar for the writing of the Apocalypse was correct, since there have been relatively few followers of the preterit scheme through

[13]Ibid.,pp. 478-83.
[14]Ibid., pp. 428-29, 432.
[15]Ibid., p. 433.
[16]Author's translation.

the Christian centuries out of the ranks of orthodox Bible-believing Christians, how yet could this purpose have been accomplished? It is presumed that if Christ's purpose was "to show" the future, then at least a goodly number of His true servants must see it. Humanly speaking, if the preterit view is the true one, the purpose of the book has not been accomplished. The preterit view simply does not harmonize with the accomplishment of this decreed purpose of God as it is stated in Revelation 1:1, and the time has long since passed for it to ever have been achieved under the preterit scheme.

Fourth, the lack of harmony among the preterists themselves; fifth, their abysmal failure to sustain their case that the body of the Apocalypse can be made to harmonize with the history of the first century of the church; and sixth, the fact that Revelation 4-19 refers to a period in the world's history that is yet future—which proposition will be later demonstrated—all combine to discredit this approach. It is therefore not strange that few believers today, if any, champion this theory which robs the church of her comfort and encouragement in knowing God's detailed plan of how evil shall be destroyed and the Kingdom inaugurated.

HISTORICAL

The historical approach, like the preterit, takes the events of the book to portray actual events in heaven and earth, but it affirms that Revelation 4-19 or 20 finds a progressive fulfillment during the course of this present church age, from the time that John wrote at c. A.D. 95-96 unto the second coming of Christ. Revelation 21-22 is assigned to the eternal state. In other words, those who espouse this view hold that Revelation 4-20 narrates the course of church history from the cross to the second advent.

Albert Barnes gives one of the most detailed and erudite expositions of this position in his commentary on the Apocalypse. It reads like a well-written volume on church history, and for this reason it is quite worthwhile. An apprehension of his system of equating Revelation 6-19 with history can be had by consulting the table which immediately follows. In light of this table certain criticisms can be leveled at Barnes's representative exposition and at the system as a whole.[17]

17Ibid., pp. iii-lxii, 31-464.

TABLE 1
Albert Barnes's Historical Interpretation of Revelation 6-19

	DESCRIPTION	BARNES'S HISTORICAL INTERPRETATION
1st seal (Rev 6)	White horse—a conqueror	Peace and triumph in the Roman Empire from Domitian to Commodus (96-180).
2nd seal (Rev 6)	Red horse—war	Bloodshed from the death of Commodus onward (193—).
3rd seal (Rev 6)	Black horse—famine	Calamity in the time of Caracalla and onward (211—).
4th seal (Rev 6)	Green horse—death	Death by famine, etc., Decius to Callianus (243-268).
5th seal (Rev 6)	Martyrs	Martyrdom under Diocletian (284-304).
6th seal (Rev 6)	Heavenly disturbances	Consternation at the threat of barbarian invasions, Goths and Huns (365—).
1st trump (Rev 8)	1/3 earth smitten	Alaric and Goths invade the Western Roman Empire (395-410).
2nd trump (Rev 8)	1/3 sea smitten	Genseric and Vandals invade (428-468).
3rd trump (Rev 8)	1/3 rivers smitten	Attila and Huns invade (433-453).
4th trump (Rev 8)	1/3 sun, moon smitten	Odoacer and Heruli conquer Western Roman Empire (476-490).
5th trump (Rev 9)	Torment of locusts	Muslim and Saracen powers rise in the East (5 months of Rev 9:5, 150 years!).

First, the hermeneutical method which is used is that of allegorization. Thus the heavenly disturbances of the sixth seal wherein "the sun became black as sackcloth of hair, and the whole moon became as blood" (Rev 6:12) are taken to be "consternation and alarm *as if* the world were coming to an end" fulfilled in the threat of the invasion by the Goths and Huns (A.D. 365 onward).[18] The grammatico-historical method of heremeneutics rejects such exegesis. The description is no doubt recorded in the language of appearance, so that we know what the sun and moon will look like at this time, and similes are used so that the sun's blackness is "as (*hōs*) sackcloth of hair" and the moon's redness is "as (*hōs*)

[18]Ibid., italics added.

Table 1 (continued)

ITEM	DESCRIPTION	BARNES'S HISTORICAL INTERPRETATION
6th trump (Rev 9)	horsemen slay 1/3 men	Turkish power rises in the East.
Angel and little book (Rev 10)	Angel gives book to John	The Protestant Reformation. The 7 thunders of Revelation 10:3-4—Papal false doctrine.
The beast and false prophet (Rev 13)	They blaspheme 42 months	The evil career of ecclesiastical and civil Rome. 42 months of Revelation 13:5—1260 years!
First five bowls are poured out (Rev 16)	Wrath by sores; seas rivers and sun smitten; darkness	The French Revolution and its aftermath strike at the Papacy.
6th bowl of wrath poured out (Rev 16)	Way prepared for armies to come to Armageddon	The frog-like spirits call paganism; Muhammadanism and Romanism prepare for their final struggle against the gospel.
7th bowl poured out (Rev 16)	Earthquake and hail; Babylon remembered for wrath	Papal power overthrown.
Babylon destroyed (Rev 17-18)	Babylon destroyed	Destruction of the Papal power.
Battle of Armageddon (Rev 19)	Christ slays the beast and his armies	The gospel finally triumphs morally over its foes who appear "as if" they are to be eaten by fowls.[19]

[19]Albert Barnes, Revelation, pp. lvi-lxii.

blood,"[20] but for us who accept the fact that God can providentially or directly work heavenly wonders, this verse can teach nothing but that heavenly disturbances will result on that day. This alone accounts for the fact that the men of earth recognize these judgments as "the wrath of the Lamb" (Rev 6:15-16). The next verse says, "for the great day (hē hēmera hē megalē) of their wrath has come" (Rev 6:17). If this impending Gothic invasion is "the great day" of prophetic wrath (cf. Jer 30:7), how can the Scriptures be true which declare that the church is not the object of God's wrath (Rom 5:9; 1 Thess 5:9) when Christians of that age suffered enormously, along with pagans, from the initial shock of

[20]Ibid.

the barbarian incursions? The answer is that on this point as on almost every point advanced by the historicist system, the alleged correspondence between the Sacred Writ and history does not meet the demands of sound exegesis of the text. Rather the exegesis is an arbitrary result of the system which demands a point-by-point chronological harmony between the Apocalypse and church history. Ellicott's suggestion that the sixth seal represents the fall of paganism under Constantine is no better.[21]

Second, the first five bowls of wrath (Rev 16) being alleged as prophesying the French Revolution and its aftermath is a typical example of the *unwarranted* rejection of the literalness of many portions of the Apocalypse by this approach.[22] These "last plagues" (Rev 15:1) of sores, the smiting of the sea, rivers, sun, and the kingdom of the Beast with darkness (Rev 16) cannot be rejected as literal events and allegorized away so easily. This is because the first bowl which inflicts sores upon the men who have the mark of the Beast (Rev 16:1-2) is very similar to the sixth plague of boils which smote the Egyptians (Exod 9:8-12); the third bowl turning the rivers to blood (Rev 16:4-7) seems identical to the first Egyptian plague except that the former is on a larger scale (Exod 7:19-21); the fifth bowl which fills the kingdom of the Beast with grievous darkness (Rev 16:10-11) is the same as the ninth plague of Egypt (Exod 10:21-23); and the hail of the seventh bowl (Rev 16:17-21) is similar to the hail of the seventh Egyptian plague (Exod 9:22-26).[23] Since the plagues of Egypt literally occurred, is it not reasonable to believe that these similar bowl plagues will in like manner come to pass?

Third, although the harmony may be worked out somewhat on a more elongated scale by men who write after Barnes (who wrote in 1851—before the two world wars, the rise of the communist powers, and the use of modern nuclear weapons), yet it is manifest that (1) the account in Revelation 6-19 does not actually yield the events of secular and church history, and (2) the events of history cannot even be fitted into the Apocalypse as the historicists attempt unless arbitrary allegorizing is permitted at every turn to do away with the plain significance of the text.

Fourth, the use of the so-called Year-Day Principle, which is

[21]Alford, 4:249 citing Ellicott.
[22]Barnes, p. lx.
[23]Clarence Larkin, *The Book of Revelation*, pp. 140-41.

almost part of the warp and woof of the historical school,[24] cannot be successfully defended. The Year-Day Principle is the historicist attempt to meet a problem. This problem is that Revelation 11-19 is dominated by "the Beast" (Rev 13:1, ff.) and the duration of the Beast's power is carefully limited by the Scripture to a term of forty-two months. Revelation 13:5 reads,

> And there was given to him [the Beast] a mouth speaking great things and blasphemies; and there was given to him authority to continue forty and two months.

The Beast, first seen in Revelation 11:7 killing the two witnesses, rises in 13:1 and is cast alive into the Lake of Fire in 19:20. Thus the problem that faces the historical interpreter is that if Revelation chapters 11-19 are dominated by a beast whose career of world power spans only 3½ years, or forty-two months (Rev 13:1, 4-8), if this is a literal forty-two months, then only Revelation 6-10 and perhaps 12, where the Beast is not mentioned by name, is left in which to fit the entire course of church history. Revelation 12 compounds the problem still more for its main event, the Dragon's persecution of the woman, is also limited to a mere 1,260 days, equaling forty-two months, or 3½ years (Rev 12:6).

In order to combat this fatal limitation it is advocated that 1,260 days (Rev 12:6) and forty-two months (Rev 13:5; 42 months multiplied by 30 days per month also equals 1,260 days) must signify 1,260 *years*. This theory, however, here has no internal warrant from the text, but is wholly a product of the demand of the historical school to extend the time periods in Revelation so that the long periods of church history can be made to fit into them.[25] So Barnes takes the five months of the locust torment of the fifth trumpet plague to represent 150 years (Rev 9:5).[26]

Fifth, the utter disagreement among the adherents of this position as to the correspondences between Revelation and history tends to discredit their entire position.

But the whole school of historical interpreters has been irretriev-

---

[24]See Barnes, pp. xi-xxviii, for advocacy of this principle by Robert Frew, the editor.

[25]Contrast this case with that of Daniel 9:20-27 wherein Daniel's seventy weeks (literally seventy "sevens") represent seventy weeks of years, 70 x 7 = 490 years. The context, esp. Daniel 9:2 and 2 Chronicles 36:21, here warrants seventy "sevens" of years.

[26]Barnes, p. 244.

ably discredited, if not by the extravagance of paltriness of its explanations, at least by their hopeless divergence from, and contradictions of, one another.[27]

Although there existed much confusion concerning the prophecies of Christ's first advent *before* he came, yet *after* he had arrived there was a general clarity, unity, and agreement among believers on this subject. How is it that after two thousand years of church history, the diversion widens as great new events occur in our modern age? The most obvious answer is that, like trying to fit square pegs into round holes, the two were never made to harmonize.

Sixth, and finally, as was said under the preterit view, it will be later demonstrated in this study that Revelation 4-19, as well as 20-22, pertain to a yet future era in the world's history and not to the interadvent period at all.

Thus, taking all of the above into account, the historical view must be rejected as a theory that does not have adequate support and that does not correctly explain the book of Revelation.

TOPICAL

The topical approach is also referred to as the cyclic or synchronous view.[28] Although there are variations within this school, generally, it understands Revelation 4-19 or 20 to consist of *parallel* visions or cycles, each of which covers the present dispensation. Each cycle is taken to represent some phase of the church's history. Hendriksen, for example, sees Revelation 1-3 as the Christ-indwelt church, Revelation 4-7 as the suffering church, Revelation 8-11 as the avenged and victorious church, Revelation 12-14 as the Dragon-opposed church, Revelation 15-16 as portraying final wrath upon the impenitent, Revelation 17-19 as showing the fall of the Beast and of the Babylon which is present in every age,[29] and Revelation 20-22 as the Dragon's doom and the victory of Christ and the church.[30] Both Hendriksen[31] and Lenski[32] are examples of those who champion this cause. Alford arranges the

[27]Lenski, p. 216 citing Milligan.
[28]Lenski, p. 217.
[29]W. Hendriksen, *More Than Conquerors*, p. 202.
[30]Ibid., p. 48.
[31]Ibid., pp. 28, 30-31, 47-48.
[32]Lenski, pp. 23-25, 214-17.

Apocalypse in parallel sections, but he confesses his lac rigid system and his own independence.[33]

Like the historical approach, this view sees the body of Apocalypse spanning all of church history, but this outlook differs in that instead of seeing a multitude of details foretold, it sees only a group of parallel trends prophesied. Thus it has two advantages over the historical school: (1) it avoids being attacked for arbitrary assignment of portions of Revelation to lone historical incidents; and (2) since almost every chapter in the Apocalypse reveals that God will triumph over evil in the end, by asserting the existence of a number of such trends this system makes a simple and plausible claim that opponents cannot easily set aside. There are, however, some severe criticisms of this method which must be noted despite the fine quality and general soundness of the men here taken as sample advocates.

First, it is highly questionable whether the book of Revelation under this scheme can be said to fulfill its avowed purpose of Revelation 1:1, "A Revelation . . . in order to show . . . the things which are necessary shortly to come to pass."[34] The relative pronoun translated, "things which" (ha) is identically translated three times in 1:19, "Write therefore the things which you saw, and the things which are, and the things which are necessary to come to pass after these things."[35]

In each case, the words things which refer to concrete, specific visions and events. If the topical method be adhered to and only trends of victory over evil are seen in Revelation 4-19 rather than prophecies of specific future occurences, how is this "A Revelation . . . of things which are necessary shortly to come to pass" (1:1)?[36] God's ultimate victory over evil had been known for ages before John wrote (Jude 14-15; Dan 2:44; 9:24), so how can the mere showing of this same truth even under various parallel visions be a "revelation" (apokalupsis), a revealing of something previously hidden? Believers have ever resisted the suggestion that Bible prophecies consist of mere trends, which the liberals claim astute statesmen could have seen in advance. The believers have vigilantly maintained that the bulk of Old and New Testament prophecy supernaturally reveals specific events with amaz-

---

[33]Alford, 4:245-49, 260-60A.
[34]Author's translation.
[35]Author's translation.
[36]Italics added.

ing detail (e.g., Isa 53:9; Psalms 22:14-18; Dan 9:27). It does not seem reasonable that this book entitled, *Revelation*, would be the one to show chiefly trends rather than specific events!

Second, this method often uses allegorization to explain many passages. Thus Lenski, though he speaks out against allegorizing from time to time, interprets the first four trumpet judgments which smite one-third of the earth, one-third of the sea, one-third of the rivers, and one-third of the sun and moon (Rev 8) as "destructive religious delusions in the whole world."[37] On the third trumpet, "and the third part of the waters became wormwood; and many men died of the waters, because they were made bitter" (Rev 8:10-11), Lenski writes, "The third trumpet makes visible the advance of religious delusion in the world which scorns the gospel."[38] This is allegorization which sees an arbitrary hidden meaning under the language of the Sacred Page. There is no textual basis for interpreting a smiting of rivers and men dying as a result of God's sending religious delusion. Though a true understanding of the details may not at this day be clear, since God once smote Egypt with remarkable supernatural plagues, including one upon the rivers (Exod 7:19-21), a physical smiting of the rivers cannot be here set aside without evidence. This is true despite the fact that the Revelation speaks in the language of appearance.

Third, the divergence of interpretation among advocates of this scheme, shows that the applying of the various passages to trends in church history is an arbitrary matter devoid of clear scriptural warrants. So, Hendriksen, who adopts this same topical system, sees the third trumpet as God's judgment in this interadvent age against evildoers through floods and water catastrophes, like the terrible Ohio River flood.[39] He sees the first four trumpets (Rev 8) as physical calamities,[40] while Lenski sees them as religious calamities.[41]

Lenski allegorizes; and Hendriksen's interpretation, that throughout our present age God will visit the wicked by natural disasters, does not meet the requirement of Revelation 1:1 that a revelation was to be given—for God's visiting the wicked through natural calamities has been known from antiquity (Isa 14:30). This can

[37]Lenski, p. 277.
[38]Ibid., p. 281.
[39]Hendriksen, pp. 143-44.
[40]Ibid., pp. 141-44.
[41]Lenski, p. 277.

only be a revelation if a specific new event or series of events is predicted.

Fourth, this mode of interpretation casts off the chronological landmarks which surround the seals, trumpets, and bowls. While more will be said on this subject later, it can here be noted that the Revelation shows that within each series of seals, trumpets, and bowls the judgments are opened one by one in order, starting at number one and concluding with number seven (Rev 6, 8, 16). Hendriksen, however, in making the first four trumpets four types of judgments through natural disasters, respectively those that affect the earth (1st trumpet), the sea (2nd), the rivers (3rd), and the heavens (4th),[42] cannot maintain that these have occurred in our present dispensation successively as the scriptural account portrays them to occur. In like manner, Lenski, who sees these same trumpets as religious delusions, denies their chronological succession. He writes,

> We do not think that the first four judgments [trumpets] are to be dated, one in an early century, the second in a later century, and the next two still later. The four effects are a gradation: bad, worse, still worse, and worst of all.[43]

Though correct concerning the gradation of the judgments from bad to worse as all will admit, this does not justify a doing away with the clear scriptural order. This order is done away with by Hendriksen, Lenski, and other followers of the topical method, not because something in the text demands its demise, but because if it is adhered to then they have to make each of their parallel series correspond to the events of church history. They then have the same task as the historical interpreters, only they must perform it with everyone of their series. They resist this because they themselves see as well as others that this cannot be done. The various series of seals, trumpets, vials, and other things cannot be made to conform with ecclesiastical history or secular history. Thus the system forces Lenski and others to adopt a saving alternative, to dispense with the chronological order of the opening of the seals, the blowing of the trumps, and the pouring out of the bowls.

Likewise, the topical system joins the historical school in doing away with the indications that the period dominated by the Beast,

---

[42]Hendriksen, pp. 141-44.
[43]Lenski, p. 277.

dealt with in Revelation 11-19, consists of only 3½ years (Rev 13:5; 11:2, 3; 12:6, 14),[44] This is done because the system *a priori* cannot devote any series of chapters to so short a period, but must leave them free to span all of church history. The problem is that there is no substantial evidence for doing this except that the life of the system demands it.

These things cannot be justified and their necessity points out the false nature of the system which requires it.

Fifth, this approach, like that of the preterit and historical, places the church on earth during "the great day (*hē hēmera hē megalē*) of their [God the Father and the Lamb's] wrath" (Rev 6:17), when the Scriptures teach that the church has been forever saved from this (Rom 5:9; 1 Thess 1:9-10; 5:9). Though some adherents of this school might evade this charge by one explanation or another, it generally is valid.

Sixth, and finally, as has been said under the previous two views, it will subsequently be demonstrated that Revelation 4-19, as well as 20-22, apply to a future day in the world's history and not to the present interadvent period at all.

Thus the topical theory must be set aside as not meeting the requirements of Revelation 4-19.

FUTURISTIC

The futuristic approach takes Revelation 4-19 to refer to the yet future seven year period of Tribulation,[45] the seventieth week of Daniel (Dan 9:20-27). Revelation 1-3 only is seen to treat this present interadvent dispensation, while Revelation 20 speaks of the thousand-year millennial reign, and Revelation 21-22 deals with the eternal state.

Before considering the relationship between the book of Revelation and Daniel's seventieth week, a few things should be noted concerning this latter time span. It is a future seven year period which is divided into two clearly marked halves of 3½ years each (Dan 9:27).[46] It is a time when God again takes up His dealings with Israel as a nation (Dan 9:20-27).

---

[44]Hendriksen, pp. 173-74.

[45]See Introduction.

[46]John C. Whitcomb, "Daniel's Great Seventy-Week Prophecy: An Exegetical Insight," pp. 1-4.

An arch-fiend of evil, a man called Antichrist, shall play the dominant role during these seven years (Dan 7:27; 2 Thess 2:3-12). He shall come out of the revived Roman Empire which will at this time be dominated by a confederation of ten kings, three of which he shall subdue forcibly (Dan 9:26; 7:19-25). He shall inaugurate the period by making a covenant with the nation Israel for seven years, but at the middle of the period he shall break his covenant and enter into the rebuilt Temple and proclaim himself as God, committing what the Scriptures refer to as "the abomination of desolation" (Dan 9:27; Matt 24:15; John 5:43; 2 Thess 2:3-4). From this time on, for the remaining 3½ year second half of this period, the Antichrist shall persecute Israel and the saints[47] with the most severe persecution ever known to the world (Jer 30:4-7; Dan 7:21, 25; 8:25; Matt 24:15-22). Finally, at the end of this period God shall destroy the Antichrist, save Israel, and set up His millennial kingdom (Jer 30:7-10; Dan 9:24, 27; 7:22, 26-27; Matt 24:29-31; Rom 11:26; 2 Thess 2:12).[48]

The truth of this system is confirmed by the harmony which it accords to the above cited Scripture passages, and it is further substantiated by the hopeless discord which results when any other explanation is attempted.[49] See Table 2 which follows for a reference chart showing some of the texts upon which the doctrine and chronology of the Tribulation are established.

---

[47]Who are these saints? Those who hold to the pretribulation rapture of the church (1 Thess 4:13-18), see them as Tribulation saints; those who, after the church is taken up to be with Christ, come to believe in the Saviour during the seven year Tribulation period. This is the writer's view and will be further commented on later. Midweek-pretribulationists also identify these as Tribulation saints, but hold that the church will be raptured in the middle of the week before the greatest period of tribulation begins (Matt 24:21). Mid- and posttribulationists allege that the rapture occurs respectively in the midst of and at the end of the seven year Tribulation period.

[47]Since already by the end of 1964 there existed 13,121,000 Jews in the world, the wicked Antichrist could slay more than did Hitler, and many millions could still be left out of the Jews to accept Christ at His coming. (Census figure from the Central Bureau of Statistics, Israel, quoted by the *Jewish Exponent*, August 27, 1965.)

[49]E.g., Barnes takes Christ, instead of Antichrist, to be "the prince that shall come" in Dan 9:26. Then, taking Christ to be the one who causes the oblation to cease in the middle of the seven years in Dan 9:27, he is forced to admit that he cannot explain the last half of the week. Albert Barnes, *Daniel*, 2:183-86, especially 185.

Table 2

The Seven Year Tribulation Period
in the Scriptures

(Not including the book of Revelation)

KEY:

A—   Antichrist
AR— Antichrist to be a Roman
A7— Antichrist's 7 year covenant with Israel
AA— Antichrist's abomination of desolation
AP— Antichrist persecutes Israel & saints
10K— 10 kings of Revived Roman Empire
3K—   3 kings of Revived Roman Empire
RR— Revived Roman Empire
TR— Temple to be rebuilt
MW—Middle of the week
IS—   Israel saved
3½—   3½ year time period
AX— Antichrist destroyed

Daniel 9:24, 26-27

24 Seventy weeks are determined upon thy people and upon thy holy city, to finish the transgression, and to make an end of sins, and to make reconciliation for iniquity, and to bring in everlasting righteousness, and to seal up the vision and prophecy, and to anoint the most Holy.[50]

26 And after threescore and two weeks shall Messiah be cut off, but not for himself: and the people of the prince that shall

AR come shall destroy the city and the sanctuary; and the end thereof *shall be* with a flood, and unto the end of the war desolations are determined.

A7 27 And he shall confirm the covenant with many for one week; and in the midst of the week he shall cause the sacrifice

TR and the oblation to cease, and for the overspreading of

AA abominations he shall make *it* desolate, even until the con-

MW summation, and that determined shall be poured upon the desolate.

[50]KJV used for these Scriptures.

38

43 I am come in my Father's name, and ye receive me not: if
A7   another shall come in his own name, him ye will receive.

Daniel 7:19-27

19 Then I would know the truth of the fourth beast, which
RR   was diverse from all the others, exceeding dreadful, whose
teeth *were of* iron, and his nails *of* brass; *which* devoured,
brake in pieces, and stamped the residue with his feet;

10K 20 And of the ten horns that *were* in his head, and *of* the
AR   other which came up, and before whom three fell; even *of* that
horn that had eyes, and a mouth that spake very great things,
3K   whose look *was* more stout than his fellows.

21 I beheld, and the same horn made war with the saints,
AP   and prevailed against them;

22 Until the Ancient of days came, and judgment was given
AX   to the saints of the most High; and the time came that the
saints possessed the kingdom.

RR   23 Thus he said, The fourth beast shall be the fourth kingdom upon earth, which shall be diverse from all kingdoms,
and shall devour the whole earth, and shall tread it down, and
break it in pieces.

10K 24 And the ten horns out of this kingdom *are* ten kings *that*
AR   shall arise; and another shall rise after them; and he shall be
3K   diverse from the first, and he shall subdue three kings.

AA   25 And he shall speak *great* words against the most High,
and shall wear out the saints of the most High, and think to
AP   change times and laws: and they shall be given into his hand
3½   until a time and times and the dividing of time.

26 But the judgment shall sit, and they shall take away his
AX   dominion, to consume and to destroy *it* unto the end.

27 And the kingdom and dominion, and the greatness of
the kingdom under the whole heaven, shall be given to the
people of the saints of the most High, whose kingdom *is* an
everlasting kingdom, and all dominions shall serve and obey
him.

Daniel 8:23-25

23 And in the latter time of their kingdom, when the trans-
A   gressors are come to the full, a king of fierce countenance, and
understanding dark sentences, shall stand up.

24 And his power shall be mighty, but not by his own
power: and he shall destroy wonderfully, and shall prosper,

AP and practise, and shall destroy the mighty and the holy people.

AA 25 And through his policy also he shall cause craft to pros-
AP per in his hand; and he shall magnify *himself* in his heart, and by peace shall destroy many: he shall also stand up against
AX the Prince of princess; but he shall be broken without hand.

Matthew 24:15-23, 29-31

AA 15 When ye therefore shall see the abomination of desolation, spoken of by Daniel the prophet, stand in the holy place,
TR (whoso readeth, let him understand:)

16 Then let them which be in Judæa flee into the mountains:

17 Let him which is on the housetop not come down to take any thing out of his house:

18 Neither let him which is in the field return back to take his clothes.

19 And woe unto them that are with child, and to them that give suck in those days!

20 But pray ye that your flight be not in the winter, neither on the sabbath day:

AP 21 For then shall be great tribulation, such as was not since the beginning of the world to this time, no, nor ever shall be.

22 And except those days should be shortened, there should no flesh be saved: but for the elect's sake those days shall be shortened.

23 Then if any man shall say unto you, Lo, here is Christ, or there; believe it not.

AP 29 Immediately after the tribulation of those days shall the sun be darkened, and the moon shall not give her light, and the stars shall fall from heaven, and the powers of the heavens shall be shaken:

30 And then shall appear the sign of the Son of man in heaven: and then shall all the tribes of the earth mourn, and
AX they shall see the Son of man coming in the clouds of heaven with power and great glory.

31 And he shall send his angels with a great sound of a trumpet, and they shall gather together his elect from the four winds, from one end of heaven to the other.

1 Now we beseech you, brethen, by the coming of our Lord Jesus Christ, and *by* our gathering together unto him,

2 That ye be not soon shaken in mind, or be troubled, neither by spirit, nor by word, nor by letter as from us, as that the day of Christ is at hand.

3 Let no man deceive you by any means: for that day shall not come, except there come a falling away first, and that man

A of sin be revealed, the son of perdition;

4 Who opposeth and exalteth himself above all that is

AA called God, or that is worshipped; so that he as God sitteth in

TR the temple of God, shewing himself that he is God.

5 Remember ye not, that, when I was yet with you, I told you these things?

6 And now ye know what withholdeth that he might be revealed in his time.

7 For the mystery of iniquity doth already work: only he who now letteth will let, until he be taken out of the way.

A 8 And then shall that Wicked be revealed, whom the Lord shall consume with the spirit of his mouth, and shall destroy

AX with the brightness of his coming:

A 9 Even him, whose coming is after the working of Satan with all power and signs and lying wonders,

10 And with all deceivableness of unrighteousness in them that perish; because they received not the love of the truth, that they might be saved.

11 And for this cause God shall send them strong delusion, that they should believe a lie:

12 That they all might be damned who believed not the

AX truth, but had pleasure in unrighteousness.

Jeremiah 30:4-10

4 And these are the words that the LORD spake concerning Israel and concerning Judah.

5 For thus saith the LORD; We have heard a voice of trembling, of fear, and not of peace.

6 Ask ye now, and see whether a man doth travail with child? wherefore do I see every man with his hands on his loins, as a woman in travail, and all faces are turned into paleness?

AP 7 Alas! for that day is great, so that none is like it: it is even

IS the time of Jacob's trouble; but he shall be saved out of it.

8 For it shall come to pass in that day, saith the Lord of hosts, that I will break his yoke from off thy neck, and will burst thy bonds, and strangers shall no more serve themselves of him:

9 But they shall serve the Lord their God, and David their king, whom I will raise up unto them.

IS

10 Therefore fear thou not, O my servant Jacob, saith the Lord; neither be dismayed, O Israel: for, lo, I will save thee from afar, and thy seed from the land of their captivity; and Jacob shall return, and shall be in rest, and be quiet, and none shall make him afraid.

Romans 11:25-26

25 For I would not, brethren, that ye should be ignorant of this mystery, lest ye should be wise in your own conceits; that blindness in part is happened to Israel, unto the fullness of the Gentiles be come in.

IS

26 And so all Israel shall be saved: as it is written, There shall come out of Sion the Deliverer, and shall turn away ungodliness from Jacob.

When the book of Revelation is compared to the Tribulation period just discussed, a number of noteworthy correspondences are discovered.

First, there is an unmistakable and undeniable correspondence between the Beast out of the sea (Rev 13:1, thērion, *wild beast*) who dominates Revelation 11-19 (who is both a kingdom and the dictator of the kingdom)[51] and the end-time fourth beast of Daniel 7:19-27 out of whom Antichrist arises. The following comparison chart, Table 3, shows this to be the case and makes the conclusion inescapable that the Antichrist, who rises out of Daniel's fourth beast and the Beast of Revelation, when he is seen and treated as the wicked human archdictator of the forces of evil, are one and the same person. J. B. Smith makes it clear that the Beast of Revelation is not only a kingdom, but also a person. On the Beast's being given in Revelation 13:5 "a mouth speaking great things," Smith declares that:

[51]The Beast is first seen in Revelation 11:7 killing two witnesses. The term "the Beast" is always to be taken in this work as referring to the beast who rises out of the sea (Rev 13:1). The second beast of Revelation, who rises out of the earth (Rev 13:11), will be spoken of by his other title, "the false prophet" (Rev 19:20).

This is another earmark identifying this beast with the fourth beast of Daniel. Dan 7:8, 11, 25. Some have understood this beast as referring to the fourth kingdom solely, and not to [the] king as head of the kingdom. However, this view is plainly erroneous from the fact that a kingdom has no mouth, neither does a kingdom "speak great words against the most High" (Dan 7:25). An image will be made of the beast. How could an image be made of a kingdom? The beast is associated with the dragon and the false prophet. Clearly the latter two are persons and the mutual relations show clearly that the beast who is mentioned between the dragon and the false prophet is a person likewise. Later the beast with the false prophet will be cast alive into the lake of fire. A kingdom is never spoken of as being cast as such into the lake of fire.[52]

Second, there is an amazing similarity between the chronology of the Tribulation period and the time indication of Revelation 11:2, 3; 12:6, 14; and 13:5. The time specifications in Revelation are as follows:

Revelation 11:2	"forty and two months"	—The Gentiles shall tread the holy city under foot for this time.
Revelation 11:3	"a thousand two hundred and three-score days"	—The two witnesses of God will prophesy until the Beast slays them (11:3-13).
Revelation 12:6	"a thousand two hundred and three-score days"	—The woman, Israel, flees from the persecuting Dragon, Satan.
Revelation 12:14	"a time, and times, and half a time"	—The woman, Israel, flees from the persecuting Dragon, Satan.[53]
Revelation 13:5	"forty and two months"	—Power was given to the Beast to continue for this duration.

At once it is seen that each of the five time declarations that are listed above are uniformly equal to one figure, 3½ years. Taking

[52]Jacob B. Smith, *A Revelation of Jesus Christ*, p. 197.
[53]The woman of Revelation 12:6, 14 is Israel; Revelation 12:1 cf. Gen 37:9-11. Satan is the Dragon; Rev 12:9. See chapter 5.

thirty days to the prophetic month, 1,260 days equal forty-two months which is the same as 3½ years. "A time and times and half a time" (Rev 12:14) is the Greek equivalent for the identical saying in Daniel 7:25, which there represents 3½ years (cf. Dan 4:25, 32). Also, since Revelation 12:14 with its 3½ "times" is the obvious equivalent of Revelation 12:6 with its 1,260 days, Revelation 12:7-13 being a parenthetical episode and verse 14 merely repeating the essential thought of verse 6 as the main narration continues, it is manifest that the 3½ "times" are identical to the 1,260 days, which in turn is equal to 3½ years!

When there are five different expressions citing the same time length of 3½ years, not that they are all necessarily coterminous, why should anyone deny that the duration in question is 3½ years? The year-day principle is advocated by the historicists because their chronological scheme *a priori* demands it,[54] and those who hold to the topical approach prefer this 3½ years to represent this entire present age of two millennia because their chronological scheme likewise *a priori* requires it.[55] The text of Revelation, however, by using various expressions, all of which add up to the same duration, seems to demand that the season in question be 3½ literal years.

Once this is accepted, it is immediately noted that a remarkable harmony exists between the Tribulation chronology and the Revelation specifications, as an examination of the prior table, Table 4, will show. The merit of the synchronism is inescapable and confirms the fact that the 3½-year time designations are indeed to be interpreted literally.

Thus in the light of the fact that the five approaches discussed previously were all seen to be inadequate; and in light of the two amazing correspondences (1) between Daniel's fourth beast, which is the beast of the Tribulation, and John's beast of Revelation 11-19, and (2) between the chronological framework of the Tribulation and the time notations in the book of Revelation, it can only be concluded that the futuristic approach, which assigns

[54]See chapter 1.
[55]See chapter 1.

Table 3

A Comparison Between Daniel's Fourth Beast and the Beast of the Revelation

Daniel's fourth beast:	Revelation's Beast:	
Comes up out of the sea (7:3)	Comes up out of the sea (13:1) Seven heads (13:1)	
Ten horns=ten kings (7:7, 24)	Ten horns=ten kings (13:1; 17:12)	
Another horn (Antichrist) becomes dominant ruler (7:24-26)	The Beast as a person (cf. 19:20) becomes a dominant ruler (17:12-13)	
	Like a leopard (13:2)	This Beast has characteristics from each of Daniel's first three beasts, lion, bear and leopard (Dan 7:4-6).
Stamped with the feet (7:7)	Feet of a bear (13:2)	
Great iron teeth (7:7)	Mouth of a lion (13:2) Scarlet color (17:3)	
Blasphemous (7:25)	Blasphemous (13:5) Dragon gives him power (13:2)	
Persecutes saints (7:21)	Persecutes saints (13:7; 11:7)	
Power for a time, times, and a dividing of a time (1+2+½= 3½ years) (7:25)	Power for 42 months (3½ years) (13:5)	
Defeated by God, who then sets up the Kingdom (7:21-22, 26-27)	Defeated by God who then sets up the Kingdom (19:11—20:6)	

Table 4

A Comparison Between the Chronology of the Seven Year
Tribulation Period and Five Chronological Specifications from
the Apocalypse

The Tribulation:	The Apocalypse:
Start—Antichrist makes a seven-year covenant with Israel (Dan 9:27).	
First Half—3½ years in length (Dan 9:27).	*Revelation 11:3*—The two witnesses of God prophesy for 42 months (3½ years) until the Beast slays them.[56]
Middle—Antichrist commits the abomination of desolation (Dan 9:27; Matt 24:15; 2 Thess 2:4).	*Revelation 13:5*—The Beast is given power to continue for 42 months (3½ years).[57]
Second Half—Antichrist persecutes Israel and the saints (Jer 30:4-7; Dan 7:25; Matt 24:15-22), 3½ years in length (Dan 9:27; 7:25).	*Revelation 12:6*—The woman, Israel, flees from the persecuting Dragon, Satan, for 1,260 days (3½ years).[58]
	Revelation 12:14—The woman, Israel, flees from the persecuting Dragon, Satan, for "a time, times, and a half time" (3½ years).[58]
End—Antichrist is destroyed by God who shall set up His Kingdom (Dan 7:22, 26-27; 8:25; Matt 24:29-31).	*Revelation 11:2*—The Gentiles shall tread under foot the holy city for 42 months (3½ years).[59]

[56]If the time of the Beast's power and persecution (Rev 13:5-8) is placed in the second half of the week, then this period must be in the first half. This is true because, at the conclusion of the second half of the week, all the foes of God are destroyed and the Kingdom inaugurated, while in contrast to this, three days *after* the end of the two witnesses' half-week testimony, they are still lying dead in the street and God's foes are rejoicing (Rev 11:7-10). See chapter 5.

[57]The era of the Beast's power must go through the persecution period, as the ability to persecute inherently demands political power and authority. Revelation 13:5-8 shows that blasphemy against God and persecution against the saints will characterize the Beast's activities during this time.

[58]The periods of intense persecution match perfectly.

[59]The treading under foot of the holy city occurs in the second half of the week after the abomination of desolation. Until this time Antichrist is keeping his covenant with Israel and not "treading it under foot" (Dan 9:27).

46

the body of Revelation (chapters 4-19),[60] to the yet-coming Tribulation period is certainly correct.

Another argument that Revelation 4-19 is dealing with a future time and not the present church age, is that in Revelation 11:9 men are seeking death and not finding it. In contrast to this there has been an ever-increasing number of suicides down through the Christian centuries.[61] Such arguments could be multiplied to the effect that the world has not yet passed through the events described in these Apocalyptic chapters. The failure of all schemes which seek to harmonize these chapters with church history testifies mutely to this truth.[62]

One objection to the futuristic view not previously touched should here be answered. Commenting on this view, Lenski argues, "Revelation has little direct value for the church prior to the last few years of its existence."[63] The answer to this lies in the fact that despite all of the mistaken views and confessed ignorance concerning this book on behalf of multitudes throughout the church age, Christians have been blessed, encouraged, and strengthened for battle and persecution all through these centuries by knowing, from the Apocalypse, that God has a plan that encompasses the worst that evil men will do, and that in the final hour God will triumph, the saints will be given an eternal reward, and evildoers will be destroyed forever. This great value of the Apocalypse for the church is not diminished one bit under the futuristic interpretation; on the contrary, it is magnified by it (Rev 1:3).

If, "I was in the spirit on the Lord's day, and I heard behind me a great voice" (Rev 1:10), means that at this point John was transported in the realm of the Holy Spirit into the future day of the Lord which includes the Tribulation period, then the futuristic position is proved. Having already established the futuristic position as the correct one, it is superfluous to this study to enter into a lengthy historical and exegetical study of this controversial text. However, the reader may consult Smith[64] and Hoyt[65] who

[60]The unity of Revelation 4-19 will be discussed in chapter 3.
[61]Smith, p. 144.
[62]See Alford, 4:251-52, whose approach sees the parallels of the topical school, for his confession of perplexity over what the 3½ years represent in Revelation and over other questions.
[63]Lenski, p. 215.
[64]Smith, pp. 319-24.
[65]Herman A. Hoyt, "Apocalypse," pp. 16-19.

strongly advocate it and Alford[66] and Newell[67] who strongly oppose it.[68] In the writer's opinion the case for this verse pointing to the Old Testament Day of the Lord and hence to the Tribulation is not well enough established so that it can be considered a proof text. Newell's point that "it is too early in the book to refer to 'the great and terrible day of the Lord' " seems conclusive when it is considered that immediately after relating these words the voice that speaks to John addresses him concerning things indisputably pertaining to this present church age (Rev 1:10—3:22).

CONCLUSION

The primary finding of this chapter has been the establishment of a general chronological framework for the Apocalypse. It has been noted that the initial section of the book, according to the outline of Revelation 1:19, "the things which you [John] saw," consists of the vision of Christ in chapter 1; the second division, "the things which are," comprises the letters to the seven churches of chapters 2-3; and the final portion, "the things which are about to come to pass after these things" (KJV), encompasses chapters 4-22. It has been seen that the main portion of this latter section, chapters 4-19, are to be understood by the futuristic approach as prophetically describing the seven year Tribulation period which even today still awaits the dwellers of the earth. Chapters 20-22 are taken as speaking of the Millennium and the eternal state.

[66]Alford, 4:553-55.

[67]William R. Newell, *The Book of Revelation,* p. 24. Newell, is, nevertheless, himself a futurist.

[68]That Revelation 1:10 speaks of the Tribulation is the view arrived at by Norville J. Rich, Sr., "The Meaning of the Phrase, 'On the Lord's Day' in Revelation 1:10," B.D. critical monograph.

Table 5
Reasons for Accepting
the Futuristic Approach

1. The Beast of Revelation 11-19 is the same as Daniel's fourth beast (Dan 7), which is that *yet future* final kingdom which is destroyed just prior to the establishment of the Kingdom of heaven.

2. The five specifications of the book of Revelation (11:2, 3; 12:6, 14; 13:5) upon study, harmonize perfectly with the time specifications and events that surround the yet future seven year period known as Daniel's seventieth week (Dan 9:27; 7:25; 12:7).

3. The futuristic approach to the Apocalypse is the only approach that harmonizes Daniel 7:19-27; 8:23-25; 9:24, 26-27; Matthew 24-25, especially 24:15-23, 29-31; 2 Thessalonians 2:1-12; Jeremiah 30:4-10; Romans 11:25-25; John 5:43; Zechariah 12:9-14; 8:23; and Jeremiah 23:5-8 into one unified eschatological program.

4. The futuristic approach is the only one that accomplishes the purpose enunciated in Revelation 1:1, "to show unto his servants things which must shortly come to pass." (The *liberal* approach denies this ability; the *allegorical* allegorizes away the things revealed; the *preterit* relegates that which is to be future to the past; the *historical* approach presents items so veiled that they cannot be identified even after they are completed; and the *topical* sees only general trends rather than future "things.")

5. The futuristic approach does not resort to unwarranted allegorization of the symbolical as well as literal details of the Apocalypse as the historical and topical views do.

6. The futuristic view yields a premillennial coming of Christ; but the topical view with its cyclic pattern placing Revelation 20 before Revelation 19 logically leads to amillennialism (Note: Alford, by his own admission, was not consistent to the topical scheme; and hence by virtue of this inconsistency and his sound exegesis of Revelation 20 he became a premillenialist).

7. In contrast to the above, all views except the futuristic view display (a) a dearth of positive proof in their favor; (b) a lack of a sound hermeneutical basis; (c) a lack of harmony among their adherents even on major interpretational items; and (d) an incapacity to yield an internally self-consistent eschatological program when combined with Daniel, the Olivet Discourse, and the other prophetic Scriptures.

2
Revelation 2-3:
The Chronological Problem
of the Seven Churches

THE QUESTION

Having established the validity of the concept that Revelation 4-22 deals primarily with events that shall follow this present age, the issue now turns to Revelation 2-3. The messages recorded in these chapters to the seven churches in the province of Asia make up the middle section of the book, "the things which are," according to the division of Revelation 1:19. The major chronological question in dispute about this portion of the Apocalypse is, Do these seven churches prefigure seven consecutive periods of church history which are to take place from John's time until Christ's second coming?[1] That is, are the seven churches not only historical and representative, but are they also prophetical? This and other issues will be dealt with in this chapter.

HISTORICAL AND REPRESENTATIVE

Today it is everywhere admitted that these seven churches were actually in existence at the time when John wrote.[2] Thus it is agreed that the seven churches were *historical*. Furthermore, since these letters were addressed to only *seven* churches in Asia Minor when it is known that others flourished there, such as those of Hierapolis and Colossae (Col 1:2; 4:13, 15-16), not to mention

---

[1]C. I. Scofield advocated this in *The Scofield Reference Bible*, pp. 1331-32.

[2]Bullinger, however, uniquely believes that these are seven Jewish congregations existing in the time of the future Tribulation. E. W. Bullinger, *The Apocalypse: The Day of the Lord*, pp. 68-71.

those beyond the province such as in Jerusalem, Antioch, Corinth, or Rome, it is seen that these churches were also *representative*. That is, these seven types of Christian congregations, each having its unique combination of spiritual assets and liabilities, stand in the place of all similar congregations so that those things that the Lord approves and disapproves in them, He likewise approves and disapproves in every other Christian church, regardless of its location.

Not only are they representative of the congregations of John's day, but it can safely be concluded that, since the same spiritual circumstances surround believers throughout this present age, the seven churches are also representative of all congregations which shall exist during the entire church age.

The fact that the number of churches selected is precisely *seven*, the number of completeness so often used in this last book of the Bible, also argues unremittingly that within these congregations, the entire church of this present era is representatively contemplated. Just as seven seals, seven trumpets, seven thunders, seven heads, and seven bowls of wrath each comprehend the complete fullness of their own sphere,[3] so must the seven churches encompass the complete fullness of the church. On this point, Alva J. McClain writes,

> The one thing upon which there seems to be general agreement is that 'seven' here speaks of a totality of characteristics. In the seven churches we have both every kind of church and every kind of member, which not only existed on earth in John's generation but also will exist throughout all ecclesiastical history. In other words, we have in the seven selected local churches a composite picture of *all* local churches on earth at any particular time.[4]

The remarkable and inordinate variety of experience engulfed within these few churches fits harmoniously with the view that they are representative congregations. Within the pale of only seven local assemblies the following types can be seen:

The church at Ephesus	—First love lost;
The church at Smyrna	—Persecuted church;
The church at Pergamos	—Faithful church which tolerates false teachers;

[3]Revelation 5:1; 8:2; 10:3; 12:3; 13:1; 16:1.
[4]Alva J. McClain, *The Greatness of the Kingdom*, pp. 446-47.

The church at Thyatira	—Church dominated by a power-ful false prophet;
The church at Sardis	—Spiritually dying church;
The church at Philadelphia	—Faithful witnessing church;
The church at Laodicea	—Lukewarm church.

Then when the sundry other circumstances recounted in Revelation 2-3 are added to these major trends within the churches, the combinations well typify the situations of all individuals and congregations within this age as well as their goals for improvement and their dangers of further lapsing. It can thus be said without difficulty that every segment within Christendom can see itself in these letters if it will but look. So the Scripture repeats *seven* times the admonition, "He that hath an ear, let him hear what the Spirit saith to the churches" (Rev 2:7, 11, 17, 29; 3:6, 13, 22, KJV). It is to be noted that the admonition addresses itself to the individual ("He that hath"—*ho echōn*) and points him to heed what the Spirit says "to the churches" plural (*tais ekklēsiais*). This strengthens the impression that the letter is not confined to only the members of the congregation directly addressed, but that the church universal is expected to profit from the descriptions and directions to these seven especially chosen assemblies that are representative of the professing church of Christ as God sees it throughout this entire interadvent dispensation. Schaff well says,

> With good reason have theologians in all ages regarded these seven churches of Asia Minor as a miniature of the whole Christian church. There is no condition, good, bad, or mixed, of which these epistles do not present a sample, and for which they do not give suitable and wholesome direction.[5]

Someone may, however, allege that the selection of these seven churches was merely due to the fact that their cities were the several postal centers of the circular postal route that served the province of Asia. To this it may be replied that even the great advocate of this theory, W. M. Ramsay, considered these seven congregations to be "constituting among them an epitome of the Universal Church and of the whole range of human life." He thought them to be representative![6] Also it must be remembered that the Lord Jesus Christ, the Author of the words to the churches (Rev 2:1 cf. 1:11-20) was not in any way limited to the congrega-

[5]Philip Schaff, *History of the Christian Church*, 1:454.
[6]W. M. Ramsay, *The Letters to the Seven Churches of Asia*.

tions of the province of Asia, much less to seven postal cities. He who had the power to choose any church, any number of churches, and who could put them in any order, did choose only those seven. He, through the inspiration of the Holy Spirit, is responsible for the order recorded; be it one that He, as God, providentially arranged to coincide with an Asiatic postal route or not.

In the shadow of the above it may at this point be concluded that:

> The churches named are selected not because of their prominence in the days of the apostles (only two—Ephesus and Laodicea—are previously mentioned in the Bible) but because of their representative character.[7]

The churches of Revelation 2-3 are not only historical, but they are also one of the representative seven of the Apocalypse. In this capacity they stand for the church of Jesus Christ on earth as He sees it, from the time of the apostles to the Rapture and the inauguration of the Tribulation events of Revelation 4-19.

PROPHETICAL

Now the question can be examined, Are these seven churches prophetical? That is, do they prefigure seven consecutive periods of church history which are to take place from John's time until Christ's second coming?

THE THEORY PRESENTED

The theory that the seven churches of Revelation 2-3 are prophetical, that they represent seven consecutive periods in ecclesiastical history, seems to have first been suggested by some of the words of the martyr Victorinus, Bishop of Pettau (died c. A.D. 303).[8] This belief as held today does not deny that at the same

---

[7]Jacob B. Smith, *A Revelation of Jesus Christ*, p. 61.

[8]Joseph A. Seiss, *The Apocalypse*, 1:128-29 citing *Migne's Patrologiae*, vol. 5, col. 320 gives the pertinent words in Latin from Victorinus's *Scholia in Apocalypsin*. However, since his commentary on Revelation has been edited by Jerome and later hands, it is difficult to determine all of Victorinus's beliefs and teachings on this topic. The seven churches represented to him the entire church catholic, he saw a special significance in the number seven, and he felt strengthened in his opinion by observing that Paul had written to precisely seven churches. Victorinus was further a chiliast.

time the seven churches are also historical and representative. It asserts that the prophetical element is in addition to these other elements and wholly compatible with them. Thus it beholds the seven congregations (1) as historically existent at the time of John's writing in A.D. 95-96, (2) as representing the entire church through the seven types of local churches which shall exist throughout the dispensation, and (3) as prefiguring seven aspects of the professing church which would successfully rise into prominence before Christ's second coming.

The seven periods are generally given approximately as follows:[9]

1. Ephesus—Apostolic church (A.D. 30-100)
2. Smyrna—Persecuted church (A.D. 100-313)
3. Pergamos—State church (A.D. 313-590)
4. Thyatira—Papal church (A.D. 590-1517)
5. Sardis—Reformed church (A.D. 1517-1790)
6. Philadelphia—Missionary church (A.D. 1730-1900)[10]
7. Laodicea—Apostate church (A.D. 1900-)

The dates given are not to be overly pressed, but are to serve as guides that point to the approximate time one era concludes and the next begins. It must be kept in mind that this theory does not claim that the entire earthly church would homogeneously pass from stage to stage. Rather it is acknowledged that during this entire interadvent era, somewhere on earth there would be persecuted churches like that of Smyrna,[11] faithful witnessing churches like that of Philadelphia, dead churches like that of Sardis, and lukewarm churches such as Laodicea. What is contended is that the dominant characteristics of the seven churches of the Revelation would rise in church history successively within the professing church in the order divinely given and that these seven periods would consume the entire interadvent age. It is acknowledged that some of the advocates of this position may state its principle differently, and by so doing inject additional ideas into

[9]Smith, pp. 61-62; Clarence Larkin, *The Book of Revelation*, p. 19; Seiss, 1:76-86.

[10]The overlap between the fifth and sixth periods is intentional.

[11]Many churches in Africa, China, Spain, and Russia have been persecuted during the last half century.

it. It is to be noted that the verdict that shall be arrived at concerning this theory as here put forth, if favorable, cannot automatically be made to incorporate the additional elements which some may propound—especially those of an extreme nature.

Hoyt, who favors the prophetical view, lists some others who adhere to it. The list is as follows:[12]

1. L. S. Harrison	15. Larkin
2. Tatford	16. Gaebelein
3. Scott	17. Hains
4. Tenney	18. DeHann
5. Morgan	19. N. Harrison
6. Seiss	20. Blanchard
7. Newell	21. Talbot
8. Ironside	22. Grant
9. Ottman	23. Pettingill
10. Kelly	24. Adams
11. Theissen	25. Simpson
12. Stanton	26. Walvoord[13]
13. Pember	27. Spurgeon[14]
14. Pentecost	

While scriptural truths cannot be settled by the mere counting of ballots or by quoting famous expositors, the list above is given so the reader can see for himself that this view is not just the dream of one or two obscurantists, but one that has been held by many prominent Bible expositors. This theory will be further clarified as arguments in favor of it are brought forward and as objections to it are examined.

ARGUMENTS IN FAVOR OF IT

The dominant aspects of the churches of Revelation 2-3 seem to rise to prominence in church history in the identical order as they are successively recorded. Furthermore, there seems to be in some cases an amazing correspondence between the details mentioned

[12]Herman A. Hoyt, "The Apocalypse," pp. 35-38. I have added items 26 and 27 to Dr. Hoyt's list.

[13]John F. Walvoord, *The Revelation of Jesus Christ*, pp. 50-100.

[14]Ibid., p. 62.

concerning particular churches of the Apocalypse and the periods of ecclesiastical history to which they are assigned.

In examining the above argument it will first be necessary to bring forward the course and main divisions of church history. Next, the successive descriptions of the apocalyptical congregations and the periods to which the prophetical theory assigns them will be compared to this course of history to determine whether or not a correspondence exists.

Church history

In order to obtain a glimpse at the path of ecclesiastical history no one better can be consulted than Philip Schaff, the dean of church historians, whose eight-volume set is world famous. He at the outset of his *magnum opus* points out concerning this topic,

> In regard to the number and length of periods there is, indeed, no unanimity: the less, on account of the various denominational differences establishing different points of view, especially since the sixteenth century. The Reformation, for instance, has less importance for the Roman church than for the Protestant, and almost none for the Greek; and while the editc of Nantes forms a resting-place in the history of French Protestantism, and the treaty of Westphalia in that of German, neither of these events had as much to do with English Protestantism as the accession of Elizabeth, the rise of Cromwell, the restoration of the Stuarts, and the revolution of 1688.[15]

With this in mind Schaff then offers his own division from a conservative Protestant viewpoint, which may be assumed to be a reliable one. His witness on this topic is especially valuable to this study since he does not state any opinion in his *History of the Christian Church* regarding the prophetical view of the seven churches.[16] His breakdown of the subject, written in 1880, is shown on Table 6 which follows.

Schaff's division may be taken as giving a highly accurate and unbiased outline of the church's progress through this present dispensation from a *human viewpoint*, and further multiplication of charts seems unwarranted for the present purpose.

[15]Schaff,1:14.
[16]Ibid., 1:450-54.

Table 6
Philip Schaff's Outline of
the Periods of Church History

Part I.   The history of Ancient Christianity from the birth of Christ to Gregory the Great. A.D. 1-590.[17]

Period 1: The Life of Christ, and the Apostolic Church. From the Incarnation to the death of St. John. A.D. 1-100.

Period 2: Christianity under persecution in the Roman Empire. From the death of St. John to Constantine, the first Christian emperor. A.D. 100-311.

Period 3: Christianity in union with the Graeco-Roman empire, and amidst the storms of the great migration of nations. From Constantine the Great to Pope Gregory I. A.D. 311-590.

Part II.   Medieval Christianity, from Gregory I to the Reformation. A.D. 590-1517.

Period 4: Christianity planted among the Teutonic, Celtic, and Slavonic nations. From Gregory I to Hildebrand, or Gregory VII. A.D. 590-1049.

Period 5: The church under the papal hierarchy and the scholastic theology. From Gregory VII to Boniface VIII. A.D. 1049-1294.

Period 6: The decay of medieval Catholicism, and the preparatory movements for the Reformation. From Boniface VIII to Luther. A.D. 1294-1517.

Part III.   Modern Christianity, from the Reformation of the sixteenth century to the present time. A.D. 1517-1880.

Period 7: The evangelical Reformation, and the Roman Catholic Reaction. From Luther to the Treaty of Westphalia, A.D. 1517-1648.

Period 8: The age of polemic orthodoxy and exclusive confessionalism, with reactionary and progressive movements. From the Treaty of Westphalia to the French Revolution. A.D. 1648-1790.

Period 9: The spread of infidelity, and the revival of Christianity in Europe and America, with missionary efforts encircling the

[17]Schaff gives "4 B.C. or earlier" as the true time of Christ's birth. Ibid., 1:111-19.

57

globe. From the French Revolution to the present time. A.D. 1790-1880.[18]

Church history and the seven churches

At this point the prophetical view may be placed beside the span of history to determine whether there exists a correlation between the churches of Revelation 2-3 and actual historical events. As no human eye can behold the course of the past two millennia and be certain it is seeing what God sees, this examination and its conclusions, whatever they might be, carry with them an unavoidable amount of subjectivism. Nevertheless the following is to be noted:[19]

Ephesus. This first church is taken to represent the *apostolic church* of the first century, A.D. 30-100 according to the prophetical view. This period of time coincides with Schaff's first period, "the life of Christ, and the apostolic church," A.D. 1-100.

Revelation 2:1-7 pictures the Ephesian congregation as one credited with works, toil, and patience, one that has rejected false apostles, and one that hates the work of the Nicolaitans. However, its fault was that it had lost its first love, its original zealousness for the Lord and His coming.[20]

This seems to harmonize well with the history of the first-century church whose original zeal and ardor is the model for all succeeding time (cf. Acts 1-28). The loss of this original fire by the time that John wrote, c. A.D. 95-96, can hardly be disputed. If, as very possible, the "Nicolaitans" (*Nikolaitōn,* vs. 6)—derived from *Nikaō,* to conquer, and *laos,* people—refers to "laity-conquerors,"[21] the hating of these sees the early church's resistance to an episcopal hierarchy and priestly caste as long as the apostles survived. The rejection of false apostles would correspond to the fact that generally the early gnostic and anti-trinitarian heresies, although started often in the first century, did not gain sweeping footholds across the land until the second and third centuries (cf. 2 Cor 11:13).[22] The Judaizing heresy was re-

[18]Schaff, 1:13-20.

[19]The reader is asked to keep in mind that, in the following discussion on the letters to the seven churches, no attempt is being made to completely exposit or exegete the passages. They are treated only insofar as is germane to the prophetical view at hand.

[20]Hoyt, p. 43.

[21]Smith, p. 64. Ignatius and Irenaeus took them to be a group who lived immorally.

[22]Schaff,1:566.

58

sisted in the first century, and then, as the face of Christendom turned more Gentile, it vanished (Acts 15; Gal 1-6).

Smyrna. This second assembly is the persecuted church, A.D. 100-313. This duration corresponds perfectly to Schaff's second period, "Christianity under persecution in the Roman empire," A.D. 100-311. Revelation 2:8-11 tells of this group's poverty in worldly things, but the group is seen as rich in God. Blasphemy from Jewish sources seems to be leveled against it. The lot of this group is tribulation and imprisonment, but Scripture specifically prophesied, "ye shall have tribulation ten days."

Certainly the imprisonment and tribulation of the Smyrna church coincides with the time of persecution in A.D. 100-313. The ten days of tribulation prophesied for Smyrna (Rev 2:10) seems to correspond to the ten primitive persecutions of Nero, Domitian, Trajan, Marcus Aurelius, Septimus Severus, Maximinus, Decius, Valerian, Aurelian, and Diocletian.[23] These have been so enumerated from the fifth century.[24] If it be said that Nero's falls before the prophetical period usually suggested, A.D. 100-313, the persecution by Julian the Apostate (A.D. 361-363) may fill in the gap. However, if Nero is included, there is an overlap with the former period; and if Julian is included, then the overlap comes with the later period. When one also considers that there were persecutions from the Arian emperors against the orthodox, he discovers with Augustine that, " it does not seem to me that the number of persecutions with which the church is to be tried can be definitely stated."[25] Schaff adds, "But the number [ten] is too great for the general persecutions, and too small for the provincial and local."[26] However, the closeness to ten as generally enumerated leaves the possibility well open that in God's reckoning the number may be precisely ten.

Revelation 2:9 speaks of Smyrna enduring the blasphemy of false Jews. This harmonizes with the following description:

> They [the Jews] caused the death of Symeon, bishop of Jerusalem ([A.D.] 107); they were particularly active in the burning of Polycarp *of Smyrna* [c. A.D. 155) and they inflamed the violence of the Gentiles by calumniating the sect of the Nazarenes.[27]

[23]Ibid., 2:33-34.
[24]Ibid.
[25]Ibid., citing Augustine in footnote.
[26]Ibid.
[27]Ibid., 2:37; italics added.

Pergamos. The third congregation is the *state church,* A.D. 313-590, and it chronologically fits Schaff's third period, "Christianity in union with the Graeco-Roman empire," A.D. 311-590. Revelation 2:12-17 informs all that this church held fast Christ's name and refused to deny His faith even though the church dwelled where Satan's throne was. One out of their number, Antipas, died as a faithful martyr among them (v. 13). The fault, however, of this assembly was that it tolerated in its midst those who held two false doctrines, Balaamism and Nicolaitanism (vv. 14-15). Those who would "hold the teaching of Balaam" are professors of the faith who, like the original Balaam, lead others to defile themselves with the sins of their pagan surroundings (Num 22-24). The Nicolaitans, hated by the Ephesian church (Rev 2:6), but here indulged, are those who seek lordship over their brethren through clerical hierarchical distinctions.

In comparison to the above, Christendom in A.D. 313-590, like the historical Pergamos church, held fast Christ's name and did not deny His faith during the great doctrinal controversies settled by the early ecumenical councils, Council of Nicaea (A.D. 325, Christ is divine); Council of Constantinople (A.D. 381, the Holy Spirit is divine); Council of Ephesus (A.D. 431, natural man is totally depraved); Council of Chalcedon (A.D. 451, Christ is human and divine); [28] and at the Second Council of Constantinople (A.D. 553, the divine-human Christ is one person).[29]

However, when in A.D. 313 Constantine made Christianity the state religion, the sacred corridors of the church began to be trampled by the defiling feet of the world with its moral corruption, and the ones who pushed to make the church more worldly were those who held the teaching of Balaam (Rev 2:14). The holders of the Nicolaitan doctrine were the men who during this time pressed for an episcopal priestly system which already by the fifth century saw Leo I (A.D. 440-461) claim that the Bishop of Rome was the successor to Saint Peter and Pope of the church catholic.[30]

It is difficult to avoid the general agreement between the Pergamos congregation as described in Revelation 2 and the years designated by the prophetical school as corresponding to this church.

Thyatira. Fourth among the churches, Thyatira is assigned to

[28]B. K. Kuiper, *The Church in History,* p. 75.
[29]Schaff, 3:351-52.
[30]Smith, p. 73.

the position of *papal church*, A.D. 590-1517. Comparing this epoch to Schaff's outline, Table 6, it is seen to comprehend all of "Mediaeval Christianity, from Gregory I to the Reformation, A.D. 590-1517." Within this time Schaff arranges three periods: (1) Christianity planted among the Teutonic, Celtic, and Slavonic nations, A.D. 590-1049; (2) the church under the papal hierarchy, and the scholastic theology, A.D. 1049-1294; (3) the decay of mediaeval Catholicism, and the preparatory movements for the Reformation, A.D. 1294-1517.[31]

The assembly at Thyatira, as told of in Revelation 2:18-29, had works, love, faith, service, and patience to their credit with their last works being greater than their first (v. 19).[32] However, they were permitting Jezebel, a false prophetess, to seduce the servants of God into fornication (v. 20). Since she did not repent when God gave her time, He promises to throw her and those who commit adultery with her "into great tribulation" *(eis thlipsin megalēn)* and to "kill her children with death" (vv. 21-23). To the others at Thyatira, "as many as have not this teaching, who know not the deep things of Satan," the Lord says, "I cast upon you none other burden," and He admonishes them to hold fast to what they have (vv. 24-25). In addition to this the Lord is here pictured as the "Son of God" with "eyes like a flame of fire" and with feet "like burnished brass"—which things portray His omniscient eyes seeing the deeds of all and His feet ready to trample the evildoers in judgment (v. 18).

In matching the description with the years A.D. 590-1517, from the year that Gregory I "the Great" became "the first of the popes" to the year Luther hung his ninety-five theses at Wittenburg in A.D. 1517, it is worthwhile to quote J. B. Smith:

> In Thyatira a woman (Jezebel) is the prominent figure. A woman in Scripture symbolizes a religious system; e.g., in the Old Testament, Israel is spoken of as the wife of Jehovah; He as her husband. Isa. 54:1, 5; Jer. 31:32. In the New Testament, the true church is the bride or wife of Christ. Eph. 5:23, 32; Rev. 19:7; 21:9. The mother of harlots is Rome. The corrupt Protestant churches, which came out of Rome, are her daughters.[33]

[31] See Table 6.
[32] Greek, *ta erga sou ta eschata pleiona tōn prōtōn.*
[33] The identity of Jezebel's children whom God shall slay, as applicable to the prophetical interpretation, can be applied to Protestant bodies only as they have become apostate. The Greek and Eastern Orthodox bodies may likewise be included as Jezebel's children in the final ecumenical apostasy.

Observe, too, that the sins of the woman, Jezebel, are similar to those of the great harlot (Rev. 17:1-6); hence the conditions prevailing in Thyatira reappear in Rome and her daughters in the latter days.[34]

Speaking on Jezebel's fornication and adultery, Smith adds that this

may be a prophetic forecast of the Dark Ages (near A.D. 1000) known as the Period of Pornocracy when popes were the playthings of vile women, one of whom posed hypocritically as a man in a man's clothing.

The bed (Rev. 2:22) also refers symbolically to "great tribulation." The reference is undoubtedly to the period preceding the coming of the Lord in power and great glory and described in chapters 6-18. *Great tribulation* [has no article], probably due to its first mention in the book, for in 7:14 it appears in the Greek with the article.

The exhortation is *hold fast till I come.* This shows plainly that the message to Thyatira is not intended merely for the local congregation at Thyatira, for it implies that she will continue in some sense until the coming of Christ.[35]

Many more things could be mentioned in comparing the system dominated by the Papacy in these years to Jezebel; the evils of superstition, immorality, pluralism, simony, and absenteeism which filled the church; the Babylonian Captivity at Avignon (A.D. 1305-1377) and the Papal Schism (A.D. 1377-1417) with their attendant evils; the Spanish Inquisition sanctioned by Pope Sixtus IV in 1478;[36] and the burning of Huss in A.D. 1415. The Lord's saying that He "gave her time that she should repent; and she willeth not to repent of her fornication" (Rev 2:21) fits the long duration which the system of Romanism has been allowed to live.

Amid these evils the commendation of the all-seeing Lord also goes out for the works, love, faith, patience, and service of Thyatira. In this, too, a resemblance is seen to the good things and the faithful believers of this period upon whom there is no further burden put upon them except for the admonition to hold fast (vv. 24-25).

Sardis. Fifth in order comes Sardis, beheld as the *reformed*

[34]Smith, p. 75.
[35]Ibid., pp. 77-79.
[36]Schaff,4:434.

church,[37] A.D. 1517-1790. This span includes, according to Schaff, two periods of modern Christianity. These are (1) "The evangelical Reformation and the Roman Catholic Reaction. From Luther to the Treaty of Westphalia, A.D. 1517-1648"; and (2) "The age of polemic orthodoxy and exclusive confessionalism, with reactionary and progressive movements," A.D. 1648-1790.[38] Thus this duration extends from Luther to the time of the French Revolution.

The portrait of Sardis in Revelation 3:1-6 is of a body that is spiritually dead despite its renowned name and its outward appearance of life. It is ordered to save the things that remain alive lest the Lord suddenly come with judgment. Its only commendation is, "thou hast a few names in Sardis that did not defile their garments" (Rev 3:4).

When this description is put beside the years A.D. 1517-1790, a special difficulty is encountered in attempting to compare the two. This is because the Sardis church was a "dead" church that *appeared* to be alive. For this very reason it is beyond fallible man's capacity, whether or not he endorses the prophetical view, to gaze at the entire spread of that day's Christendom and then to dogmatically assert that the church as a whole was or was not a dead church that appeared to be alive.

At A.D. 1517, however, the church does seem to meet this specification. Both the Western Catholic and the Eastern Orthodox[39] bodies were in stagnation though their power, ritual, and long standing made them *in the eyes of many* appear to be alive. In fact today some still look at such centuries with admiration, especially the earlier thirteenth century, which marks the height of papal power.

The "few names in Sardis that did not defile their garments" (Rev 3:4) is a description most applicable to the reformers and their followers who obeyed the injunction, "establish the things that remain, which were ready to die" (Rev 3:2).

Yet, it is not impossible that the Sardis message may be just as suitably applied to the end of the period, c. 1750-1790, at the time preceding and during the French Revolution. Here the Roman, Eastern, and Protestant bodies all appeared alive to their own adherents, yet the religion and morality that came to be exhibited

[37]This title is here used not to denote the Calvinistic churches, called "Reformed," but to indicate the era of the Reformation and its extended aftermath.
[38]See Table 6.
[39]The schism between the Latin and Greek churches took place in A.D. 1054.

during the 1700's in the skepticism of the Enlightenment, English deism, and the atheistic surge of the French Revolution showed that even the Protestant segment of the professing church was largely dead in Christ's eyes. Here the command, "establish the things that remain" (Rev 3:2), fits the circumstances of the Great Awakening which took place c. 1730-1800.

Dead Catholicism saved in part by the Reformation and dead Protestantism saved in part by the Great Awakening both separately and together fit the message to Sardis.

Philadelphia. From A.D. 1730-1900 is the sixth church. Schaff describes the time between 1790-1880 as "the spread of infidelity, and the revival of Christianity in Europe and America, with missionary efforts encircling the globe."[40] The scriptural account referred to this time, Revelation 3:7-13, contains a message to the Philadelphia congregation which is devoid of criticism. This group's works are known by her Lord, she has a little power, she has not denied Christ's name, and an open door which none can shut is set before her (Rev 3:7-8). Christ promises to this group that He will make the false Jews of the Synagogue of Satan worship at their feet (v. 9). He also pledges that

> because thou didst keep the word of my patience, I also will keep thee out of the hour of trial which is about to come upon the entire inhabited world, to try the ones dwelling upon the earth. I come quickly" (Rev 3:10-11).[41]

The above narration's lack of any mention of evil in the church makes this sixth letter, prophetically speaking, refer to only the good elements in the church of the eighteenth and nineteenth centuries. The Great Awakening on both sides of the Atlantic with its Whitfield and Wesley (c. 1730-1800) was followed by a Second Awakening in the 1800's with its revivals, camp meetings in America, and its men like Moody and Spurgeon.[42] The worldwide missionary movement of the 1800's saw messengers of Christ travel to the ends of the earth with the tidings of good news.[43] This fits the Philadelphia church who, with its little power, remained faithful to Christ's name in two centuries of increasingly outspoken infidelity. The open door pictures well the unparal-

[40]See Table 6.
[41]Author's translation.
[42]Kuiper, pp. 442-49.
[43]Ibid. The first American missionaries were ordained in 1812 at Salem, Mass.

leled opening for missions which was so earnestly used during the entire nineteenth century.[44]

This situation fitly depicts the rise that came out of Christendom between the deadness of the Sardis period, ending at about 1790, and the evils and laxness of the Laodicean era, which begins somewhere about 1900. An overlap is necessary, and since the prophetical view acknowledges that all seven types simultaneously persevere unto Christ's coming despite the rise into prominence of one church after another, the overlap is in complete harmony with the theory.

The promise of Revelation 3:10 to keep the Philadelphia church "from the hour of trial, the hour which is to come upon the whole earth" need not, according to the prophetical theory, be applied to the faithful living in 1730-1900. Rather it is to be applied to those in the "Philadelphia category," true believers, who are alive during the final Laodicean period that will end with the rapture. For, remember, the prophetical theory rightly enunciated maintains that Christendom will until Christ comes always contain Christians and congregations of all seven of the representative types—however, a different type will dominate each of the seven eras. Thus it is quite within the pale of the theory to understand Revelation 3:10 to call for Philadelphia Christians to be raptured at the close of the Laodicean age.

In examining the Greek of Revelation 3:10, several items are discovered favorable to this interpretation. The words "out of the hour" (ek tēs hōras) show that Christ will keep those to whom the promise is directed outside of (ek) a specific ("the"—tēs) time period ("hour"—hōras; cf. John 2:4). This period, "the hour of trial" is one of "trial" or "temptation," both of which senses are conveyed by the word peirasmos.[45] It is further noted that this same word for "trial," used here in Revelation 3:10, is used in Luke 8:13. However, when the passages exactly parallel to Luke 8:13 are consulted, Matthew 13:21, Mark 4:17, it is seen that the "trial" of Luke 8:13 (peirasmou) is described in Matthew 13:21 and Mark 4:17 as "tribulation or persecution" (thlipseōs ē diōgmou). Thus the understanding of "the hour of trial" as a definite time period of tribulation is seen to have warrant when the text is studied. This period is to affect the "entire inhabited world."

[44]Ibid.

[45]William F. Arndt and F. Wilbur Gingrich, A Greek-English Lexicon of the New Testament and Other Early Christian Literature, p. 646.

When all of the above factors are put together in light of: (1) the fact that a specific future Tribulation period of seven years yet awaits the earth;[46] and (2) the absence of evidence for the promise of this verse ever having been fulfilled in the history of the historical Philadelphia congregation;[47] a notable case is made for this verse promising a pretribulational rapture according to the claim of the prophetical school's advocates.[48]

Laodicea. The seventh and final congregation sets forth the final season of the church from 1900 to the rapture. This phase in history has so far seen two world wars, the rise of the international communist conspiracy since 1917, the Korean conflict, and in the last few years the war in Vietnam, the wars in the Middle East, and a world wide wave of political revolutions and upheavals hitherto without parallel. In the religious world it has seen in China, Africa, Soviet dominated Asia, and in other places throughout the world, more martyrs for Christ than in any previous century. Liberalism, neo-orthodoxy, unbelief, and skepticism have invaded the church to the extent that many of Protestantism's largest denominations openly deny the fundamentals of the faith. Yet, as always a remnant remains true according to the election of grace (1 Kings 19:18; Rom 11:2-5).

Revelation 3:14-22 unfolds the Laodicean assembly as one neither hot nor cold and therefore about to be spewed out. It thinks itself to be rich, but in the penetrating sight of Christ it is wretched, miserable, poor, blind, and naked. Yet it is encouraged to accept this chastening as an act of love, and to therefore repent.

It is hard to escape the impression that a correlation exists between the above description and the lukewarmness on the part of today's professing church. In the face of today's rise and spread of atheistic communism, which now threatens all the world, much of Christendom calls for peace at any price. The Bible is put out of United States public schools, and clergymen who call themselves Christian support the act. Ethical standards are being cast away for moral relativism; few clergymen raise their voices against it; and some clerics have become so corrupted that they even cham-

[46]See chapter 1.

[47]See Albert Barnes, *Revelation*, p. 95.

[48]So Walvoord, pp. 86-90, and Smith, pp. 87-90. Anyone, however, who espouses the view that the seven churches are representative, can believe that Revelation 3:10 promises a pretribulational rapture without necessarily endorsing the prophetical view.

pion the new immorality with a brazen lip and glib voice. Unbelief and skepticism are found to thrive within Protestantism's portals, and the believers in denominations so overrun call for no discipline. Prominent Protestants are calling the Reformation a mistake and the ecumenical movement is seeking union with Rome. Homicide is on the increase, and clergymen call capital punishment murder. Sin has so abounded that it is no longer beheld with horror and dread. The attitude of Christendom in a world of growing infidelity is one of lukewarmness!

Preliminary conclusion

Comparisons have been made above between the biblical accounts of the seven churches and the periods in church history which they are said to represent. On the basis of these it must be said at this point that the validity of comparisons have much in their favor; the dominant characteristics of the seven congregations do appear to rise in church history successively in an order identical to that given in Revelation 2-3.

Do the seven stages, however, as the theory also avers, consume the entire duration of the interadvent age? They do if (1) the uniformly suggested pattern of arranging the periods alongside of church history is correct so that these present days are the final Laodicean days, and if (2) this present period is concluded by Christ's coming for His church rather than by any worldwide revival that would eliminate this age from being the final Laodicean period and would necessitate a reappraisal of the entire scheme. Yet with today's global increase of infidelity based on the false humanistic presupposition that modern science has disproved the existence of God and the supernatural, it seems safe to say that there will be no such worldwide, lasting revival to end our age. Nothing is seen on the horizon which can reverse the trend except the coming of Christ (2 Pet 3).

Other arguments

Biblical names often have special significance, like Adam, Eve, Abraham, Isaac, Israel, and Jesus. In like manner it is urged that the names of the seven churches providentially match the spirit of the seven ages they represent and hence provide another argument in favor of the prophetical theory. Jacob B Smith, a Greek scholar most noted for his *Greek-English Concordance to the New Testament,* gives the following meanings for the congregational names:

> Ephesus means "let go" or "allow," hence "declension" or "relaxation";
> Smyrna means "bitter";
> Pergamos from *pergos,* "a tower," hence "elevation," and *gamos,* "marriage";
> Thyatira from *thuos,* "sacrifice" and *ateires,* "unweary," hence "unweary of sacrifice";
> Sardis. The Hebrew word *sarid,* meaning "the rest or remnant," is the probable source of Sardis;
> Philadelphia means "brotherly love";
> Laodicea derived from *laos,* "people" and *dike,* "judgment," hence "judgment of the people."[49]

So Ephesus is the age when the first love is "let go" or "relaxed"; Smyrna is the "bitter" period of persecution; Pergamos is the time of the church's "elevation" to a favored religion and hence the time when it is "married" to the evil "world"; Thyatira is the long season of Rome's domination when continuous works and masses saw it "unweary of sacrifices"; Sardis is the era when the living "remnant" is rescued from the dead mass; Philadelphia is that surge when "brotherly love" was shown in Christ's name by evangelization and missionary zeal; and lastly, Laodicea stands for the final day when standards are determined by the "judgment of the people" in an effort to offend no one, thus yielding "democracy in religion" and a nauseating lukewarmness.

It should be further noted that the general and almost uniform agreement among the many advocates of this theory, in contrast to the discord among historical interpreters of the Revelation, commends itself as indicating that there exists some real basis behind this view.

Also, the fact that the Apocalypse is preeminently a book of prophecy ("the words of the prophecy," Rev 1:3; "the words of the prophecy of this book," Rev 22:18) and one of symbols, make the uncovering a prophetical sense in the seven letters something which cannot be thought as strange or unusual.

[49]Smith, pp. 62, 65, 70, 75, 81, 85, 91.

The three main objections to this theory are (1) that it lacks any supporting evidence; (2) that it does away with the doctrine of the imminent return of Christ; and (3) that the text does not anywhere contain any explicit statement telling its readers that these seven churches prefigure seven movements which comprehend the entire history of the church and that therefore the original readers of the Apocalypse would fail to see such a hidden prophecy.

The first objection, that the prophetical view lacks any supporting evidence, finds expression in the words of Buswell who says,

> The notion that the seven letters were intended for seven stages in church history, as given in the paragraph headings in the Scofield Reference Edition of the Bible, must be understood as fanciful and speculative.[50]

This objection must be put aside forthwith on the basis of the examination of the previous pages. There are too many sound expositors who hold this position and too many remarkable correspondences between the letters and history to call the grounds for this opinion "fanciful and speculative."

On the second objection, that it does away with the doctrine of the imminent return of Christ (Matt 24:36, 42-44), it should be first noted that those who support this prophetical view of the seven churches are believers in the Lord's imminent return, like Smith, Scofield, Newell, Pentecost, Hoyt, Ironside, Larkin.[51]

The doctrine of the imminent return is seen not to be destroyed if one remembers that no one could see all seven divisions except possibly those alive after the final division had been in progress for some time, and to those the coming would still be imminent as Christ could be expected by them to come at any moment. Thus a person alive at A.D. 150 could not boldly say, "I am living in the Smyrna period and therefore Christ cannot come now"; for without our present historical perspective of two thousand years and without the infallible mind and eyes of God, this person would have no way of being certain that he was not living in A.D. 150 in the last days of the Laodicean period. The prophetic view merely declares that whenever the Lord comes, had it been in A.D. 150 or

---

[50]J. Oliver Buswell, Jr., *A Systematic Theology of the Christian Religion*, 2:428.
[51]Ibid.

whether it be in A.D. 2150, all seven stages will by then have transpired. There was never any biblical commitment that required the interadvent age to extend for its present two millennia, so there was never anything to prevent the seven steps from taking place in seven hundred years, seventy years, or even seven years if the plan of God had so arranged events. Thus the understanding of the seven churches here at issue, does not do away in any sense with the imminency of the blessed hope of the church, Christ's return.

The third objection, that the text does not itself explicitly assert that the seven churches contain a prophetic preview of the church age and that its original readers would fail to see such hidden prophecy, is answered by two observations.

McClain supplies the first observation toward this objection. He writes:

> For the true explanation may be that in the seven churches of the Apocalypse the Holy Spirit did give a *latent* revelation of the Church's career on earth, but so obscure that it could not be clearly discerned until the last or Laodicean era had been reached. If so, it would be significant that only in modern times have many devout Bible students come to agree that there was such a revelation and that we are now living in the final era of the Church on earth. Such a method of revelation is not novel in Scripture; for the Second Advent of our Lord could not be certainly identified in Old Testament prophecy until the First Advent had been realized in history.[52]

The second observation which answers the objection is made by Hoyt. After noting that the Protoevangelion, Genesis 3:15, promises that the seed of the woman would bruise the serpent's head, Dr. Hoyt traces the progressive unfolding of this prophecy through Scripture. The Redeemer would come from the line of Shem (Gen 9:18-27). He would be of Abraham's seed (Gen 12:1-4), He was to be of Judah's tribe (Gen 49:8-10), of the family of Jesse (Isa 11:1-5), of the line of David (2 Sam 7:12-13), out of Bethlehem (Mic 5:2), and from the virgin (Isa 7:14). On the basis of this Hoyt remarks,

> None would ever have dreamed that Gen. 3:15 would have unfolded exactly in this way. It must then be concluded that there was

[52]McClain, p. 449.

70

more in that simple statement of Gen. 3:15 than at first meets the eye. Such we believe true of the seven letters to the seven churches.... Only as the picture is unfolded is it possible to look back and see how much was wrapped up in those amazingly simple reconstructions of the future.[53]

CONCLUSION

The seven congregations were first seen to be both historical churches and ones representative of the types of Christians and congregations that would be in existence continually throughout this age until the return of the Lord. In addition, on the strength of striking correspondences observed between the history of the church and the seven churches of the Revelation which seem to be beyond chance; and on the basis of the lesser argument noted above, including the understandings brought out in light of the objections; it is herewith concluded that there was indeed a latent prophecy of the course of the church age placed in Revelation 2-3. Thus the churches seem to be *historical, representative,* and *prophetical.* However, because of the nature of the case, this conclusion cannot be made with the dogmatism that is characteristic of the enunciation of other more fundamental scriptural truths.

[53]Hoyt, pp. 37-38.

3
Revelation 4-5:
The Chronological Problem
of the Throne Scene

Revelation 4-5 presents a breathtaking scene. The Father is manifested upon the throne surrounded by a rainbow, the four living creatures are next about the throne, then come the twenty-four elders, then the myriads of angels, and finally as the concentric circles grow even larger all other creatures in the universe are seen. Christ, the Lamb, takes the book with the seven seals from the Father and all the universe breaks out in rapturous song and shouts of holy joy.

The questions to be dealt with in this brief chapter ask, "What is the chronological relationship between the event signified by this magnificent vision and the Tribulation period?" and "What is the relationship between this event and the rapture of the church?"

THE THRONE SCENE AND THE TRIBULATION

UNITY AND FUNCTION OF REVELATION 4-5

It was previously concluded in the first chapter of this study that Revelation 4-19 pertains to that future seven year Tribulation period which is otherwise known as Daniel's seventieth week. At that time it was assumed that chapters 4-19 comprised a unity and no special effort was made to elaborate on this. At this point, however, it is proper to actually note the precise affinity that Revelation 4-5 bears to 6-19 so that the chronological connection between these two sections may be exposed.

This unity between Revelation 4-5 and the chapters of the Apocalypse which follow is pointed out by comparing Revelation

4:1 with 1:19. Revelation 1:19 divided the book into three sections, "the things which you [John] saw" (the vision of chapter 1), "the things which are" (the things pertaining to the church age, chapters 2-3), and "the things which are about to come to pass after these things." In light of this the voice of Revelation 4:1 informs John that he is now about to see "the things which are necessary to come to pass after these things," he is about to be shown the things that make up the third division of the book. The words in Revelation 1:19 that signify this third and final section of the book are, in the Greek, almost identical to those in 4:1, and the meanings of the two expressions clearly represent the same thing.

> Revelation 1:19, "the things which are about to come to pass after these things" (ha mellei genesthai meta tauta)[1]

> Revelation 4:1, "the things which are necessary to come to pass after these things" (ha dei genesthai meta tauta)[2]

This means that Revelation 4-22 forms a unity consisting of the things to come after the church things of chapters 2-3.

The type of unity that Revelation chapters 4-5 bears to chapters 6-22 must be seen by observing the subject matter of these sections. Starting backwards, Revelation 21-22 is seen to deal with the inauguration of the eternal state; chapter 20 treats the thousand year millennial reign of Christ; chapters 6-19 deal with the Tribulation period and its plagues of seven seals, seven trumpets, and seven bowls of wrath; and Revelation 4-5 shows the scene in which Christ takes the seven-sealed book[3] from the Father. The opening of the seals of this book by Christ begins the plagues of the Tribulation which start with the opening of the first seal at Revelation 6:1.

Thus the scene of Revelation chapters 4-5 may be thought of as the anteroom which stands before the Tribulation period. It is the showing of the Lamb obtaining "the title deed of the universe."[4] This sealed deed is a writ of repossession and eviction. Sin and Satan have usurped the creation with millions of its inhabitants from the holy God, but Christ, by dying, became able to salvage the earth so that the original holy purpose could be fulfilled. Only

---

[1]Author's translation.
[2]Author's translation.
[3]Actually a scroll (biblion).
[4]So Herman A. Hoyt, "Apocalypse," p. 105.

He who paid the price and defeated sin is worthy to evict Satan and all sinners from their illegal domain (Rev 5:2-5) and to repossess the creation for God. The longsuffering of God and the Lamb is now over (2 Pet 3:9; Rev 6:16-17). Christ will now, starting at 6:1 with the first seal, progressively open the deed, and as He does so judgments of rising intensity will be let loose (Rev 6-19) until the sinners are destroyed and God again maintains actual possession of His world (Rev 20).

CHRONOLOGICAL LOCATION OF REVELATION 4-5

It is clear that the scene of Christ taking the book from the Father represents an act which takes place after the cross and before the Tribulation begins. It is before the Tribulation begins manifestly because the Tribulation only starts when Christ opens the first seal of this book (Rev 6:1). Since the sacred account demands that the book be in the Saviour's hands before He opens it (Rev 5:1-6; 6:1), it is impossible for anyone accepting chapters 6-19 as the Tribulation period to dispute the point that the taking of the book by Christ must occur prior to the start of the Tribulation.

It is equally clear that the Saviour takes the book from the Father after the cross. This is because His suffering on the cross is declared as the basis for His being worthy to receive and open the book. So the hosts sing in Revelation 5:9, "Worthy art thou to take the book, and to open the seals thereof: for thou wast slain, and didst purchase unto God with thy blood men of every tribe, and tongue, and people, and nation."

The question, "How much time prior to the start of the Tribulation period does the Son receive the sealed book?" may now be asked. In answer to this it is to be noted that the vision that John saw in Revelation 4-6 finds no indication of any sustained length of time elapsing between the Son's reception of the book (Rev 5:7) and His opening of its first seal (Rev 6:1).

If this receiving and opening of the book had occurred immediately after the ascension, it should properly have been expected to be shown in Revelation 1 as part of the vision of the risen Christ. Since, however, this scene is located in the third section of the Apocalypse that unfolds "the things which are about to come to pass after these things" (Rev 1:19; cf. 4:1 which starts section three), its place is after the "church things" of Revelation 2-3, or at the minimum according to any view after John's writing, which was done years after the ascension. If it was not directly after the ascension then it must be at the only other appropriate time, right before the beginning of the Tribulation.

This conclusion is seen to be a necessity in the wake of Chapter 1's discovering that the futuristic approach was the correct one in opposition to the historical and other views. For if the seven-sealed book was opened by Christ and if the Tribulation which it unleashes was begun at either the ascension or at c. A.D. 95-96 when John saw and penned the Apocalypse, then the historical approach is manifestly correct. But, since the futuristic approach was seen to be the true one, the opening of the seven-sealed book and the releasing of its frightful contents can commence no earlier than at the start of the future Tribulation period.

The rainbow and lightnings which accompany the Throne of Adjudication[5] set in heaven (Rev 4:2-3, 5) further confirm the view that the opening of the sealed book is associated with a period of judgment such as the Tribulation rather than with the ascension of the original time of John's vision. The rainbow round about tells of mercy in the midst of divine wrath (Gen 9:8-17) and the "lightnings and voices and thunders" which proceed out of it symbolize God's presence *coming nigh* for the judgment of sinners (Exod 19-16ff; Rev. 8:5; 11:19 cf. 15:5-6; 16:18).[6]

The act of the Son's receiving the book from the Father likewise should not be thought to consume anything but a relatively short time. This is because this act is a mere ceremony based on a past labor, the cross (Rev 5:9), and it is not itself pictured as any long process or arduous task. Although the Son may have waited the entire present age before taking the book because of God's long-suffering (2 Pet 3:9), there is no reason why the ceremony should have taken two millennia. If it is argued that He has been progressively taking this book during the present age, it must be answered that this is to relegate this present period to the position of a necessary prerequisite to Christ's taking the book when the account expressly declares that the cross was the only requirement (Rev 5:9).

[5]This is Newell's title for the throne. William R. Newell, *The Book of The Revelation*, pp. 85-89.

[6]In each of the occurrences of lightnings and thunderings in the book of Revelation a more intense judgment is about to fall on the impenitent or one has just been completed.

All of this corroborates the belief that Christ receives the sealed book directly prior to the Tribulation and forthwith commences to open it, letting loose its various divine visitations of wrath. There is, however, yet another facet of this subject to be examined before the above opinion may be regarded as being established. This topic will now be studied under the heading below.

THE THRONE SCENE AND THE RAPTURE

Final conclusions with regard to the chronological placing of the throne scene should be delayed until its relationship to the time of the rapture of the church is at least considered. One's view of the time of the rapture is generally interwoven with his identification of the twenty-four elders of Revelation 4-5. If the twenty-four elders who participate in the throne scene represent the church already raptured, then this ceremony which John witnessed must take place in the brief interval between the rapture (1 Thess 4:13-18) and the start of the Tribulation (Rev 6:1). Also if this be the case, the rapture must necessarily be a pretribulational one for the church is already seen wearing crowns in heaven before the outpouring of wrath begins. Much, therefore, depends on the identity of these elders.

As search is made to determine exactly who they are, many clues are seen to be offered in their description in chapters 4-5. Their number is twenty-four, they are sitting, robed in white raiment, and wearing golden crowns which they cast before the throne in adoration (Rev 4:4, 10-11). They have harps and golden vials filled with the prayers of the saints (Rev 5:8), and in Revelation 5:9-10 they say to the Lamb,

> Worthy are you to take the book and to open its seals, for you were slain and you redeemed to God by your blood some out of every tribe and tongue and people and nation, and you made them unto our God a kingdom and priests, and they shall reign upon the earth.[7]

In comparing the above characteristics of the elders with pertinent or similar Scriptures the following is noted: (1) the redeemed out of humanity are pictured as having been robed in white raiment (Rev 3:5; 6:11); (2) elders are the representatives of the people in the local churches of which they are overseers (Acts

[7]Author's translation.

20:17, 28; James 5:14); (3) elders represented the Jewish nation in synagogue and government in John's lifetime (Matt 15:2; 16:21); (4) the New Testament promises believers victor's crowns (*stephanos*—the same word as in Rev 4:4, 10) in 2 Timothy 4:8; James 1:12; 1 Peter 5:4; Revelation 2:10; 3:11; (5) those who participate in the first resurrection will be priests of God and shall reign with Christ (Rev 20:6); (6) twelve is the "governmental number," there being twelve tribes in the Old Testament and twelve apostles in the New Testament—a total of twenty-four; (7) twenty-four courses of priests, with a head man for each, was the structure of the Aaronic priesthood that represented all Israel (1 Chron 24:3-5); and (8) the twelve apostles were promised that they would sit on twelve thrones and judge the twelve tribes of Israel (Matt 19:28; Luke 22:30).

When the characteristics of the twenty-four elders are compared to the eight similar factors listed above, which are found elsewhere in Scripture, certain conclusions may be drawn. The elders of the throne scene are certainly seen to be representatives of redeemed men, and they are either twelve representatives of the Old Testament saints and twelve representatives of the New Testament saints, or all twenty-four represent the New Testament church. Buswell questions this and says,

> The "twenty-four elders" are *not* necessarily representative of the ransomed in heaven, for the first person plural of the pronouns in Revelation 5:9, "Thou hast redeemed us ... we shall reign upon the earth" [KJV] is not well substantiated in good manuscripts. These two verses are spoken *of* the redeemed by the twenty-four elders in the third person and the prediction is, "They will reign upon the earth." Whatever the elders represent, they add to the impressiveness of the scene.[8]

To this criticism two replies must be made. First, the disputing that the elders are representatives of the ransomed on the grounds that the words "us" and "we" which appear in the King James Version of 1611 do not appear in the best texts is not the coup de grace of this view. A comparison with the translation of these verses, Revelation 5:9-10, made earlier on page 76 from the best modern Greek text shows that representatives of the redeemed could indeed well say these words.[9] If one will examine these

[8]J. Oliver Buswell, Jr. *A Systematic Theology of the Christian Religion*, 2:429.
[9]Eberhard Nestle; Erwin Nestle; and Kurt Aland, *Novum Testamentum Graece*, Revelation 5:9-10.

verses and recall that all the apostles personally were Jews just as were the twelve patriarchs for whom Israel's tribes were named, he can see that the usage of the third person may be most suitable on the basis of the twenty-four elders probably personally being all Jews. If this be true, then, "you redeemed ... *some* out of every tribe and tongue and people and nation," actually fits the situation better than, "you redeemed ... *us* out of every tribe and tongue and people and nation." This would be correct whether they represent both Old and New Testament saints or New Testament ones alone. In any case, while the usage of the first person pronouns as in the KJV would clearly establish the case that these represent the ransomed, the usage of the third person pronouns does nothing to contradict it.

Second, Buswell's comment, "Whatever the elders represent, they add to the impressiveness of the scene," tends to have the effect of casting the quest for their identity into the realm of the subjective and unknowable when their characteristics have points which correspond clearly to the redeemed. Their title and number, "twenty-four elders," (*presbuteroi*) shows that they are representatives of some group or groups; their white raiment points to their having been redeemed; their being seated on thrones and wearing crowns means that they have emerged victorious out of some struggle; and the golden bowls filled with the prayers of the saints which they carry link them with the saints. Since they are clearly never identified as *angels, and* since all angels in the book of the Revelation seem always to be identified as such, the twenty-four can hardly be angels. Besides, their position as elders and their crowned condition, does not fit the angels.[10] What is left? Everything points to the same conclusion, that they are representatives of the ransomed saints gathered in glory, either of both the companies of the Old and New Testament saints together or of the New Testament redeemed alone.[11] In

[10]Walvoord, *The Revelation of Jesus Christ,* p. 107, describes the unusual view of Stonehouse that the twenty-four are angels though he himself, Walvoord, does not support it. The traditional view and the conviction of almost all of the commentators has ever denied that the twenty-four could be angels.

[11]At Christ's return *for* His church, the believers then alive without ever dying will be raptured along with all those "dead in Christ" (I Thess 4:13-18; I Cor 15:51-52). The "Tribulation saints" are those who, after the rapture, accept Christ during the actual Tribulation period. Those of this latter group who remain alive at Christ's coming *with* His church at the end of the Tribulation will enter the millennial Kingdom (Matt 25:34).

either case the New Testament saints are represented as seated and crowned in heaven, their struggle being a thing of the past.[12]

From this, in the words of Walvoord, an inescapable conclusion follows:

(1) "If the twenty-four elders of Revelation 4:1-5:14 are representative of the church, as many expositors believe, it would necessitate the rapture and reward of the church before the tribulation."[13]

With this are combined other arguments for a pretribulation rapture such as:

(2) None of the New Testament passages on the Tribulation mention the church (Matt 24:15-31; I Thess 1:9-10; 5:4-9; Rev 4-19).

(3) The translation of the church (I Thess 4:13-18; I Cor 15:51-52) is never mentioned in any passage dealing with the second coming of Christ after the Tribulation.

(4) The church is not appointed to wrath (Rom 5:9; I Thess 1:9-10; 5:9). The church therefore cannot enter "the great day of their wrath" (Rev 6:17).[14]

(5) The church of Philadelphia was promised deliverance from "the hour of trial, that hour which is to come upon the whole world, to try them that dwell upon the earth" (Rev 3:10).

(6) It is characteristic of divine dealing to deliver believers before a divine judgment is inflicted upon the world as illustrated in the deliverance of Noah, Lot, Rahab, etc. (2 Pet 2:6-9; see especially Gen 19:22).

---

[12]For a complete study of this matter, see John P. Burke, "The Identity of the Twenty-Four Elders of Revelation 4:4," B.D. critical monograph.

[13]John F. Walvoord, *The Rapture Question*, p. 197.

[14]In connection with this argument, if the midtribulationists were correct that the rapture takes place at the sounding of the seventh trumpet, then the church as a body would experience, at a minimum, much of the fury of the first six trumpet soundings as well as the effects of the seals. Cf. Rev 6:16-17 which shows that men realize that the events of the sixth seal convey the wrath (orgē) of God.

Norman B. Harrison, The End: Re-Thinking the Revelation, pp. 111-12, takes violent exception to calling the seals and trumpets "judgments." He does this because as a midtribulationist he believes the church to be upon the earth during the opening of the seals and the blowing of the trumpets, until the blast of the seventh trumpet. Therefore believing that the church will not come under God's "wrath" or "judgment" (Rom 5:9), he seeks to prove that neither the seals or trumpets are judgments of God's wrath.

However, Rev 6:17, "For the great day of His wrath is come," said concerning the sixth seal, and left uncorrected proves Harrison to be in error.

(7) The pretribulational interpretation is the only view which teaches that the coming of Christ is actually imminent.[15]

(8) 2 Thess 2:7, as interpreted by many expositors, indicates that the presence of the Holy Spirit as He indwells the believers is the force holding back the manifestation of evil which is yet to come at the end of this age. Thus the rapture of the church must occur before the Antichrist and the Tribulation can overtake the world. If any should ask, "But how or in what sense can a person of the all-present Godhead be taken from the earth?" the answer must be that in the same special sense that the Comforter came upon earth (John 15:26; 16:7) He will again depart at the rapture. If then it is asked, "Then how can those saved during the Tribulation (Rev 7:14, Greek, "the great tribulation") be saved?" the answer must be that these will be saved in the same way that the Spirit in the Old Testament by grace saved men.

(9) 2 Thess. 2:1-5 indicates a pretribulation rapture. Here Paul argues "by the coming of our Lord Jesus Christ" (v. 1) that the Thessalonian Christians were not yet in "the day of the Lord" (v. 2),[16] i.e., the Tribulation period. He adds that the great "apostasy," the "falling away" from the faith had to precede this period of judgment (v. 3) in order to prepare the way for "the man of sin,"[17] the Antichrist (v. 3). In verse 5 Paul reminds the Thessalonians that he had already told them these things when he was with them. If the things which Paul had taught them are further indicated in the First Epistle to the Thessalonians we see then that he taught them of the rapture when Christ would come for His Church (1 Thess 4:13-18) and of the period which Paul called "the day of the Lord" which Paul in 1 Thess 5:2-4 described as a time when "sudden destruction would fall upon an unsuspecting evil world. Paul here must be speaking of that period described by Christ in Matt 24:21, that is, the Tribulation. Thus the force of 2 Thess 2:1-5 is that by the fact that the rapture is yet to occur you cannot now be in the Tribulation period (v.

[15]These first seven arguments are taken from "Fifty Arguments for Pretribulationism," Walvoord, The Rapture Question, pp. 191-99.

[16]The oldest Greek manuscripts have in 2 Thess 2:2 the words "the day of the Lord" rather than "the day of Christ" as the KJV has because it followed in 1611 the latter Byzantine manuscripts which were available at the time.

[17]Literally: "the man of the lawlessness."

2) which also must be preceded by the great apostasy (v. 3) which will prepare the way for the coming of the Antichrist (v. 3).

(10) If "the falling away" (hē apostasīa) of 2 Thess 2:3 signifies the rapture rather than the end-time "apostasy," which is the view of some scholars (e.g., E. S. English, A. A. MacRae), according to this verse, the Rapture must occur before "the day of the Lord," the Tribulation, spoken of in I Thess 5:2-4.

Thus a cumulative argument exists that by Revelation 4, before the start of the Tribulation, the church has been raptured into heaven and is seen in John's eyes in the twenty-four elders.[18]

The argument that the call to John by the trumpet-like voice of the Lord in Revelation 4:1, "Come up hither," is a type of the church being summoned to the rapture, and that since it occurs at this point it must be a pretribulational one, is advanced by Larkin and others.[19] While there is a strong coincidental element here that cannot be laughed at, yet the argument does not seem to have sufficient weight behind it for even many pretribulational advocates to offer it as one of the many proofs for their case.[20] It is interesting, it is remarkably coincidental, it can be put forward with some degree of merit, but as a proof text it cannot rise above the question mark which surrounds it.

CONCLUSION

The investigation conducted in this chapter strongly favors the Son's receiving the seven-sealed book from the Father immediately before the Tribulation period begins. This heavenly, symbolical ceremony is performed in the presence of the saints of this present age who are in heaven. This favors a pretribulational rapture of the church, which body is seen by the apostle in the persons of the twenty-four elders.[21]

---

[18]For a fine defense of the pretribulation view, see Gerald B. Stanton, *Kept from the Hour: Biblical Evidence for the Pretribulational Return of Christ.* Also see Newell, pp. 382-405.

[19]Clarence Larkin, *The Book of Revelation,* pp. 32-34; Hoyt, p. 99.

[20]E.g., Walvoord, *The Rapture Question,* pp. 191-99.

[21]It is beyond the scope of this study to attempt to give a full scale rebuttal of the midtribulation rapture position. The student who is interested in an answer to such claims is referred to J. Dwight Pentecost, *Things to Come: A Study in Biblical Eschatology,* pp. 179-92.

Let it be noted, however, that in partial reply to the argument that the seventh trump blows in the middle of the seven years *and* that it is the "last trump" (1 Cor 15:52), and therefore the trumpet of the rapture, that Matt 24:29-31 shows that at least one trumpet will sound after the seventh trumpet. Since the trump of Matt 24:31 plainly comes after the Tribulation, and hence after both the seventh and the rapture trumpet, the sounding of the trump of the rapture cannot be thought of as the "last trump" in time. It is better thought of as the "last trump" that marked the Roman legion's leaving its camp. Paul, remember, was a Roman citizen and one who had much contact with its military (Eph 6:11-17; 2 Tim 2:3-4).

4

Revelation 6-19: Are the Seals, Trumpets, and Bowls Contemporaneous or Successive?

Part A

INTRODUCTORY OBSERVATIONS

THE IMPORTANCE OF THE QUESTION

Having established that Revelation 6-19 deals with the seventieth week of Daniel, the future seven year Tribulation with two 3½ year halves, it is now proper to seek out the additional noteworthy chronological scaffolding of this section.

It is at once observed that three sets of judgments dominate these chapters, those of the seven seals, the seven trumpets, and the seven bowls of wrath. These three sets of seven plagues are presented in the book of Revelation in the order given above. Interspersed among them we find periodic interruptions showing explanatory and enlightening inset scenes—between the opening of the sixth and seventh seals are seen the visions of the sealing of the 144,000 and the great multitude saved out of the Great Tribulation (Rev 7).[1] This being the case, before any serious attempt can be made to assign the various plagues, inset visions, and other phenomena to a definite chronological position within the seven year Tribulation period, it is necessary to determine whether the seals, trumpets, and bowls are three series running contemporaneously as some maintain, that they all begin, run, and end together; or if they rather occur successively as others aver, the

---

[1]The Greek text of Revelation 7:14 has the definite article "the" before the words "great tribulation" (ek *tēs thlipseōs tēs megalēs*, literally, "out-of the tribulation the great-one"); cf. KJV.

seals come first, then follow the trumpets, and finally come the bowls. A correct answer to this question will aid greatly in unraveling the chronology of the seven year Tribulation, but an incorrect answer will lead only to countless erroneous concepts. All possible combinations of successions and synchronisms among the seals, trumpets, and bowls must be whittled down until the true order is reached.

The difference between (1) the first of the seven bowls of wrath being poured out *after* the seven seals and seven trumpets have already been loosed, and (2) this same first bowl being opened at the outset of the period *at the same time* when the first seal and first trumpet are being started is a profound difference indeed. The immensity of the diversion is as if in a battle, the question should be confused as to whether the air force, tanks, and infantry should each attack one after another in that order only when each preceding element has been fully committed or whether they should all begin the onslaught at the same moment. This issue must be settled positively if an internal chronology of Revelation 6-19 is to be realized.

Other possibilities, such as the continuance of the effects of some of the judgments after new ones are released so that there are overlaps, must be considered whether it is found that the three sets of plagues are in fact opened successively or contemporaneously.[2] However, the main issue must first be settled before the details are aligned.

WHOSE TESTIMONY MAY BE HEEDED?

When the question of the three series of judgments being successive or contemporaneous is discussed, as always, biblical evidence is decisive. Nevertheless, it is to be observed that although this question is dealt with by interpreters of many schools (futuristic, topical, historical, and preterit), their conclusions, analyzations, and reasonings on this topic may be heeded as far as these prove to be consistent with biblical revelation, logic, and truth. Thus an advocate of the historical scheme, which has been shown to be a false method of understanding the Apocalypse, may be correct in advocating the successive nature of the three series of judgments, if this be the case; and an advocate of the futuristic

[2]The words "judgments" and "plagues" are here used synonomously to refer to the seals, trumpets, and bowls (cf. Rev 15:1; 16:1).

scheme, the correct one, may be incorrect in advocating that the series are contemporaneous. That is, it is possible to have men holding the truth on this point whose basic comprehension of the chronology of the Revelation is incorrect, and it is likewise possible to have men holding false views on this question whose basic understanding of the book is quite accurate. With this kept in mind, the reader will not think it overly strange to see an argument or objection of a man previously refuted on other issues brought up on the present question. Of course, topical adherents will always argue for these judgments being contemporaneous for it is part and parcel of their theory that the seals, trumpets, and bowls all happen simultaneously.[3] Likewise historical advocates will uniformly see the three sets of plagues as being successive.[4]

ABOUT THE PERIOD IN GENERAL

Before plunging into the examination of the time factors involved in the various sets of judgments it is fitting for the sake of clarity that a word here be said about the general nature of this section of the Apocalypse. McClain well sums up the matter when he declares,

> Regardless of the numerous and wide differences of opinion as to details of interpretation, there should be no disagreement regarding at least three general features of this section of the Apocalypse: First, it presents a period of divine judgment and wrath poured out from heaven upon a world system which is opposed to God and His Christ (4:2; 6:15-17; 11:18; 15:1, 4; 16:7; 17:1; 17:7; 18:3-10). Second, these judgments appear in three series of seven each: seven seals (6:1-17; 8:1); seven trumpets (8:1-9:21; 11:15-19); and seven bowls or vials (15:1—16:21); the last vial being followed by a voice, saying, "It is done" (16:17). Third, within the entire period there appear some clear and striking correspondences with certain divine judgments predicted in the Old Testament and also by Christ Himself, as preparatory to the establishment of the Mediatorial Kingdom on earth.[5]

CONTEMPORANEOUS OR SUCCESSIVE?

The main questions now to be answered are: (1) Are the events

[3]E.g., W. Hendricksen, *More Than Conquerors: An Interpretation of the Book of Revelation*, p. 48.

[4]E.g., Albert Barnes, *Revelation*, pp. lvi-lxii.

[5]Alva J. McClain, *The Greatness of the Kingdom*, p. 450.

within each of the major series of seals, trumpets, and bowls contemporaneous or successive? and (2) Do the three series run contemporaneously through the entire Tribulation period or do they successively follow one after another in the order in which they are presented in the Revelation, seals first, trumpets second, and bowls third?

Part B
SUCCESSION WITHIN EACH SERIES

Before inquiring as to the relationship among the three series, the order *within* each set may first be established.

WITHIN THE SEALS

Their succession. Christ is seen opening the seven seals one by one in succession in Revelation 6 and 8. Ordinal numbers that indicate succession ("first," "second," "third," *mian, deuteran, tritēn,*) are used. Here it must be remembered that the God who knew the things to come inspired the writer of the book of Revelation to record visions and scenes that would rightly show how events would occur. It would have been an easy matter for God to have let John see seven seals released all at once if this would have best conveyed the program of the future. Likewise, the results of the seals indicate a progression of events that could be expected if they were opened one by one starting with the first: Antichrist,[6]

---

[6]In the context of the Tribulation period, Daniel's seventieth week (Dan 9:20-27), futuristic commentators almost unanimously, and correctly, take the rider on the white horse of the first seal to be the mock Christ, the Antichrist (cf. Rev 19:11). He, the Antichrist, will inaugurate his meteoric Tribulation period activities at the start of the seven years by making a seven year covenant with Israel (Dan 9:27). Preterit, historical, and topical interpreters who start Revelation 6 at the cross naturally take this to be Christ Himself (cf. Rev 19:11). In objection to this it can be said with Swete that: "the two riders [that of the first seal (Rev 6:2) and Christ in Rev 19:11] have nothing in common beyond the white horse; the details are distinct; contrast the *diadēmata polla* ["crowns many"] of xix. 12 with the single *stephanos* ["wreath-crown"] here, and the *hromphaia oxeia* ["sword sharp"] with the *toxon* ["bow"]. A vision of the victorious Christ would be inappropriate at the opening of a series which symbolizes bloodshed, famine, and pestilence." (Henry B. Swete, *The Apocalypse of St. John*, p. 86.)

That the rider, astride the white horse, begins holding a bow *(toxon)* and is crownless, favors his being a military leader who has yet to win his "victor's wreath-crown" *(stephanos)*. This crown is then given to him as he starts his ride. Starting *with* a bow but *without* a crown does not fit Christ, the conqueror of death (Rev 1:18), who Himself will give out crowns before the Tribulation begins (Rev 2:10); but it perfectly fits the Antichrist.

war, famine, death, martyrdom, and heavenly signs (Rev 6). The order of the first six seals well fits the order that these events would providentially follow. The *Antichrist* and other false leaders (first seal) will excite the nations; the aroused kingdoms will plunge into *wars* (second seal); following the ravages of war, *famine* develops (third seal); and famine and disease next increase the toll of *death* (fourth seal); then in the wake of this havoc scapegoats are sought out and murdered (*martyrs*—fifth seal); and finally, God through heavenly signs shows His wrath upon the murderers of His martyrs (sixth seal).

Kent points out that the order of the loosing of the seals in Revelation 6 presents an "amazing correspondence" to the happenings related in the Olivet Discourse in Matthew 24:4-14, which he feels to be also dealing with the Tribulation, "many ... saying, I am Christ" (Matt 24:5—cf. first seal, Antichrist); "wars and rumours of wars" (Matt 24:6—cf. second seal, warfare); famines (Matt 24:7—cf. third seal, famine); "famines and earthquakes" bringing death to multitudes (Matt 24:7—cf. fourth seal, death); and, "Then they shall deliver you up unto tribulation and shall kill you" (Matt. 24:9—cf. fifth seal, martyrdom).[7] Here note, however, that Matthew 24:4-14 may actually describe the course of this present age, starting in verses 4-8 with a period called "the beginning of sorrows" (v. 8) and culminating with events (vv. 9-14) that find their crescendo in the Tribulation period itself.[8]

Another argument in favor of the seals being opened in successive order rather than all at one time is that they reach a climax in the sixth and seventh seals. The sixth seal shows heavenly signs so remarkable that the wrongdoers on the earth cry to the rocks to fall upon them and to hide them from the face of God and from the wrath of the Lamb; they acknowledge that the great day of His wrath is come (Rev 6:12-17). Then at the opening of the seventh seal there is such a sight comprehended by the heavenly host that there begins an ominous and awesome silence in heaven that lasts for one half hour (Rev 8:1). If all the seals occurred together, it would seem strange indeed to see men killing God's martyrs (fifth seal), while at the same time begging the rocks to fall upon them.

---

[7] Homer A. Kent, Jr., "Matthew," *The Wycliffe Bible Commentary*, p. 972. This correspondence of events further points to the first seal's being Antichrist and not Christ.

[8] Cf. Luke 21:10-11. Luke 21:12-24 explains what will take place before the Tribulation.

Of course one can defend the maxim, "anything is possible," with some success, but our quest is to determine (1) what *best* fits the biblical facts and evidence and (2) what is highly improbable *and* without scriptural or logical warrant.

If it be found further on in this study that the seven trumpets come out of the seventh seal, and that the trumpets actually follow the seals in time [and this is the case as will be demonstrated in the next part of this chapter], then there exists a conclusive argument in favor of the seventh seal being the last of the seals, and therefore, the seals being opened in consecutive numerical order—rather than all being let loose at one time.

Thus the arguments favoring the seals being opened one by one, and not all at once are that: (1) the seals are clearly pictured in the biblical account as being opened successively by Christ rather than simultaneously; (2) ordinal numbers, which by their very nature convey the idea of succession, are used to enumerate the seals; (3) the order of the events of the seals coincides generally with the historical unfolding of similar demagogue-war-famine-death patterns; (4) the order of the events amazingly corresponds to the sequential order enumerated in Matthew 24:4-14 of the Olivet Discourse —yet the significance of this is a highly involved question; (5) the seals build to a climax which is reached only in the sixth and seventh seals; and that (6) *if* the trumpets come out of the seventh seal and follow the seals in time [which will be shown in the next part of this chapter], then the seventh seal is assuredly last in a consecutive order. These reasons are especially compelling since there is no scriptural passage found anywhere that requires that all the seals be opened at the same time. Thus, our conclusion must be that indeed the seals are set loose by Christ, one by one, successively, in numerical order, beginning with the first and concluding with the seventh. In fact most historical and futuristic commentators take this for granted.

Duration of the Seven Seals. The nature of the seals prevents any declaration that the effect of one seal stops completely when another starts. False agitators, especially the Antichrist (first seal) who clearly continues throughout the height of warfare and martyrdom (second and fifth seals); and warfare and famine (second and third seals) would continue during the time of the escalation of the death toll (fourth seal). Thus the opening of each seal must portray the coming of a zenith of that judgment or the time when it forcibly begins to be felt on the earth during during the seven year Tribulation period. The outworkings of each opened seal, therefore, are seen to continue on during and after the unloosing of later judgments. Revelation 6:8 decisively confirms this. It shows that the elements of the second and third seals, warfare and famine, actively take part in producing the death of the fourth seal. Revelation 6:8 says, "and it was given to them [death and hades] authority over the fourth part of the earth, to kill by the sword and by famine and by death and by the beasts of the earth.[9]

Thus the sword, which is essentially warfare, and famine, the elements of the second and third seals, are chief among the means of executing the fourth seal's decree. From this verse there can be no question that the various effects of the opening of each seal continue on in time while yet other seals are being set loose. This truth will be further confirmed when in the next chapter it is seen, that the demagoguery of the Antichrist (first seal), death (fourth seal), and martyrdom (fifth seal) continue to flourish throughout the entire Tribulation.

The exact chronological placing of the opening of the seven seals in relation to the Tribulation period will be examined later. At this point, however, it can be said that at least some brief interval of time, be it a matter of days, weeks, or months, must intervene between the opening of each successive seal. This is true because the first five seals are seen to contain providential-type judgments.[10] Such judgments are those which God, in His holy and wise control of all things in the world, permits to rise up out of natural causes. Therefore, since these judgments rise out of natural circumstances, they take time to develop. Thus the demagoguery of the first seal would need at least a little time before it could incite the warfare of the second seal. Likewise, the warfare would need a period to bring famine (third seal), and warfare and famine in turn would require at least a brief duration to yield the great death of the fourth seal.

The sixth seal, with its sun becoming black, stars falling, and cries of men in terror of God (Rev 6:12-17), is observed to be not a solely providential judgment as its five predecessors, but a more direct manifestation of divine power. This being true, God could open it at any time, however, since it has been placed as sixth it

---

[9]Author's translation.
[10]Herman A. Hoyt, "Apocalypse," p. 124.

seems that God withholds its heavenly symbols of divine wrath until after the slaying of His martyrs has been perpetrated during the fifth seal. On this movement from seal to seal Smith gives his opinion that "The first six seals follow in what appears to be a short time and in rapid sequence."[11]

Naturally none of these seals portray the absolute beginning of any of these evils on the earth for there have ever been antichrists (1 John 4:3—though not *the* Antichrist), wars, famines, deaths, martyrdoms on this planet since the Fall. Rather the seals portray the final torrential manifestation of these judgments at the end of the age, the Tribulation.

Conclusion. In light of the above it must be concluded that Christ opens the seals one by one in their numerical order, and that at least a short interval of time intervenes between the dispatching of each one. Once each seal is released its effects continue on during and after the beginning of other later judgments.[12]

WITHIN THE TRUMPETS

Their Succession. In the case of the trumpet judgments it is unquestionably clear that they are seven successive visitations of God, rather than seven portions on one synchronous catastrophe. As with the seals, the biblical picture shows the trumpets blown one after another (Rev 8; 9; 11:15). Ordinal numbers, which signify succession as opposed to coincidence, are likewise used. However, besides these general factors, the various sayings of the heavenly voices explicitly point to succession in these judgments. After the fourth trumpet, but before the fifth, are heard the words,

> Woe, woe, woe, to the ones dwelling upon the earth by reason of the rest of the voices of the trumpet of the three angels who are about to sound! (Rev 8:13)[13]

After the fifth, but before the sixth, the voice cries, "The first Woe has departed: Behold yet come two Woes after these things" (Rev 9:12).[14] Then again, between the sixth and seventh, a voice

---

[11]Jacob B. Smith, *A Revelation of Jesus Christ*, p. 126.

[12]The case of the seventh seal is unique and will be considered in detail later in this chapter when the question is raised as to whether or not the seven trumpets come out of the seventh seal.

[13]Author's translation.

[14]Author's translation.

90

cried, "The second Woe has departed: Behold the third Woe is coming quickly" (Rev 11:14).[15] In all three of the above sayings the intent of the message is that a certain number of judgments are already past while more fearful visitation is soon to come. The Greek word, apēlthen, "[it] has departed," is identically used in Revelation 9:12 and 11:14, cited above, showing clearly by its meaning that the first and second Woes respectively had decisively departed before the next Woe had entered.

If doubt lingers, Revelation 10:7 should settle it. This verse reads,

> But in the days of the voice of the seventh angel, when he should be about to sound [his trumpet], also the mystery of God should be finished, as He announced to His own servants the prophets.[16]

At this point, without going into issues involved in this verse which are not germane to the present subject, it can be seen that "the mystery of God" was to be finished in connection with the blowing of the seventh trumpet's blast. This unquestionably signifies that this seventh trumpet is the final one to sound in a temporal series.

Duration of the Seven Trumpets. As to the duration of the trumpets, the fifth trumpet's description gives an important clue. Revelation 9:5 tells that the torment of this fifth judgment should last for five months (mēnas pente). From this lone exact time specification it can be surmised that the other trumpet visitations will likewise last over a duration probably best specified in a low number of months.

Do the sayings, "The first Woe has departed: Behold yet come two Woes after these things" (Rev 9:12) and "The second Woe has departed: Behold the third Woe is coming quickly" (Rev 11:14), signify that in the case of the first and second Woes, the fifth and sixth trumpet punishments, that they will each cease before the next one commences? Surely the word, apēlthen, "[it] has departed," with the promise of the imminency of the next trumpet, shows that at the least the main thrust and force of these Woes must be spent before the next one starts. However, their after-effects no doubt remain and continue to affect the earth dwellers for some time. The fact that the torment of the fifth trumpet, the

---

[15]Author's translation.
[16]Author's translation.

first Woe, is said to last for five months (Rev 9:5) sets a definite temporal limit to the active life of at least this one plague.

The character of the first four trumpet afflictions, however, also points to judgments which occur during a definite rather limited period of time although their effects would linger on for some duration. These first four trumpets consist of: hail and fire burning one-third of all grass and trees (first trumpet); a great mountain of fire cast into the sea, turning one-third of the sea into blood and killing one-third of its creatures (second trumpet); a great burning star called "Wormwood" which makes a third part of the rivers bitter and causes many men to die (third trumpet); and a third part of the sun, of the moon, and of the stars becoming darkened (fourth trumpet). Thus the falling fiery masses which descend from the sky would be spent after a brief while, though their results might linger for years.

Conclusion. Thus the trumpet judgments are seven successive divine visitations that afflict those inhabitants of earth who do not have the seal of God upon their forehead (Rev 9:4). The judgments each seem to occur in a limited time period, although their aftermath no doubt lingers on for a considerable span.[17]

WITHIN THE BOWLS

Their Succession. The seven bowls[18] of wrath enumerated in Revelation 16, like their predecessors the seals and trumpets, are also observed to be poured out one by one successively rather than all of them merely being poured out at once into the same maelstrom. Both the biblical portrait that shows them set loose one by one in this manner (Rev 16), and their consecutive listing by ordinal numbers, the nomenclature of succession, argue for this.

Also, since under the plague of the first bowl the members of the Beast's kingdom are given a "grievous sore" (*helkos kakon*— Rev 16:2) and at the time of the outpouring of the fifth bowl, with

[17]As in the case of the seventh seal, the seventh trumpet poses certain unique problems and will be dealt with later in connection with the question, "Do the seven bowls proceed out of the seventh trumpet?"

[18]*Phialē* means a "bowl" (William F. Arndt and F. Wilbur Gingrich, *A Greek-English Lexicon of the New Testament and Other Early Christian Literature,* p. 866). The ASV calls these "bowls," but the KJV refers to them under the designation, "vials." Both English translations are acceptable.

its affliction of darkness, they are blaspheming God because of "their sores" (tōn helkōn autōn—Rev 16:11), it is apparent that the fifth bowl follows the first in time. The first bowl shows the original giving of the sores and the fifth depicts the later suffering from them. This shows that the first five bowls follow one another in relatively rapid succession.

The case is confirmed when it is noted that when the seventh bowl is released a great voice shouts, "It is done" (gegonen—Rev 16:17). This can only indicate that the seventh bowl marks the end of a series of successive judgments. Most writers correctly take the element of succession in the unloosing of these bowls for granted, so Barnes, in line with his historical system of interpretation, cites them as "the successive blows by which the Papacy will fall" (italics added).[19]

It may be noted that under the sixth bowl the call is given to the nations to come up to the battle of Armageddon (Rev 16:12-16), which takes place at the very end of the Tribulation as this period's closing scene (Rev 19:11-21). Thus while the sixth bowl is poured out before the seventh, its final effects do not take place in time until the very conclusion of the period, after the vast damage of the seventh bowl has been done, when Christ comes at His Revelation.[20]

Indeed, though the bowls may follow one another with great rapidity, and though the effects of the former ones may endure while later ones are yet being overturned, they are certainly successive.

Duration of the Seven Bowls. On the words of Revelation 16:11, already discussed above, which tell of the Beast's followers suffering at the time of the pouring of the fifth bowl from the sores of the first bowl, Alford comments,

> These words bind on this judgment to that of the first and following vials, and shew that they are cumulative, not simply successive. The sores, and pains before mentioned, are still in force.[21]

Clearly here, again, the effects of each bowl continue on while the contents of subsequent bowls are being spilled upon the earth. Jamieson, Fausset, and Brown's commentary styles the work of the bowls as "swift and sudden," and alludes to Bengel's words in

[19]Barnes, p. 356.
[20]Herman A. Hoyt, lecture, Grace Theological Seminary; Winona Lake, Ind.
[21]Henry Alford, *The Greek Testament*, 4:356.

a conjectural comparison between the interval that separated the Egyptian plagues and the time lapse between the outpouring of each of the bowls. In this fashion it notes that,

> The Hebrew thought the Egyptian plagues to have been inflicted with but an interval of a month between them severally (Bengel, referring to *Seder Olam*).[22]

Conclusion. Whatever the precise interval between the various bowls may be, and Scripture nowhere seems to indicate it, they are certainly poured out successively with at least a brief space separating the starting point of each. After each is let loose, as in the case of the seals and trumpets, its effects tarry while other later bowls are ushered forth. In this way, using Alford's term, the judgments are "cumulative" in their effect.[23]

Thus we have now seen that *within* each of the three series in Revelation 6-19, namely, the seals, trumpets, and bowls, the judgments are released successively (first one, then two, next three, etc.), and that their effects are cumulative, with the preceding judgments more or less remaining in effect as each new one is set forth.

Part C

ARE THE SEALS, TRUMPETS, AND BOWLS SUCCESSIVE?

Having established that *within* each of the three series, the judgments fall, one by one, in numerical succession, we now focus upon the relationship *among* the series. Topical advocates such as Lenski, Hendriksen, and Alford have already been seen to favor the synchronization of the three sets so that the seals, trumpets, and bowls are all seen to be unleashed and running simultaneously.[24] On the other hand, futurists, such as Buswell,[25] Hoyt,[26]

---

[22]R. Jamieson, A. R. Fausset, and D. Brown, *Commentary Practical and Explanatory on the Whole Bible,* p. 1571.

[23]Alford, 4:356.

[24]See chapter 1.

[25]J. Oliver Buswell, Jr., *A Systematic Theology of the Christian Religion,* 2:430-34.

[26]Hoyt, "Apocalypse," pp. 107a-10.

McClain,[27] Newell,[28] Pentecost,[29] and historical interpreters like Barnes,[30] aver dogmatically that the three series are not released simultaneously, but successively in the order: first the seals, second the trumpets, and third the bowls. Even though this study has already found the futuristic mode of understanding the Apocalypse to be the correct general approach, it now must be determined if its advocates are likewise right in affirming that the three series of visitations successively follow one upon another.

THE BIBLICAL PRESENTATION

A Caution. It is proper to start this inquiry by looking at the account of the Bible itself in order to learn how the scriptural narrative overtly portrays the coming forth of the various visitations from God. Then, next, the arguments of men may be considered. Buswell gives sound advice for the inauguration of this examination when he writes,

> I would urge, at this point, the avoidance of any *a priori* assumptions as to the interpretation of the material given. In particular, I wish to protest against a very prevalent assumption that the book of Revelation is built upon a principle of repetition, or that the seals, trumpets, vials, and many other portions, are to be regarded as synchronized and more or less simultaneous. There is no *a priori* ground for assuming simultaneity, and there is no *a priori* ground for denying it. The question is, What does the text say of its own form of organization?[31]

The Prima Facie Impression. When one turns to the sacred page, one finds the opening of the seals treated in Revelation 6:1 and 8:1, the blowing of the trumpets recorded in Revelation, 8, 9, and 11:14-19, and the pouring out of the bowls related in Revelation 16. From this sequential presentation alone the impression is received that the three series are chronologically set loose in a succession identical to their order of mention. When the narrative is carefully examined further, the picture of succession remains.

[27]McClain, p. 456.
[28]William R. Newell, *The Book of The Revelation*, p. 102.
[29]J. Dwight Pentecost, *Things to Come: A Study in Biblical Eschatology*, pp. 359-64.
[30]See Table 1.
[31]Buswell, 2:430.

After Christ opens the seventh seal there is a half hour of awesome silence in heaven, and then the seven angels are given the seven trumpets (Rev 8:1-2). Since the contents of the seventh seal is nowhere explicitly mentioned, unless it be the seven trumpets, and since also the seven trumpets are seen immediately after the opening of the seventh seal, the impression is that the trumpets are indeed the contents of the last seal—for otherwise there is nowhere any contents of that seal seen (Rev 8:1-7ff). The earthquake of 8:5 cannot be the content *per se* of the seventh seal, for it is clearly the precursor of the trumpet judgments. The earthquake appears in the midst of the narrative dealing with the trumpets, after all mention of the seventh seal proper has ceased (Rev 8:1-7ff).

Then when the seventh trumpet is sounded, the heavenly temple[32] of God is *opened–from the* open temple come seven angels carrying the seven last plagues, the bowls of wrath (Rev 11:14-19, cf. 15:5-8). This movement from (1) the blowing of the seventh trumpet, to (2) the opening of the heavenly temple, to (3) the coming forth out of the temple of the seven bowl angels, is a relatively direct one in Scripture. The picture of this, however, is somewhat clouded because the interluding inset episodes of Revelation 12-14 are parenthetically injected *between* (1) John's first sight of the heavenly temple opened in Revelation 11:19, right after the seventh trumpet has sounded, and (2) his second sight of the same opened temple with the seven bowl angels coming out of it (Rev 15:5-6). Omitting the elements that are more or less parenthetical, the scriptural movement is recorded as follows:

> The second Woe has departed: Behold the third Woe is coming quickly. And the seventh angel sounded: and there occurred great voices in heaven.... And the heavenly temple of God was opened, and the ark of His covenant was seen in His temple, and there occurred lightnings and voices and thunderings and an earthquake and great hail.... And after these things I saw, and the temple of the tabernacle of the testimony in heaven was opened, and the seven angels, the ones having the seven plagues, came out of the temple (Rev 11:14-15, 19; 15:5-6).[33]

Here in the case of the seventh trumpet, as with the last seal, if the seven bowl angels do not comprise the content of the "Woe"

[32]The inner sanctuary (*naos*).
[33]Author's translation.

of the final trumpet (Rev 11:44), then there is nowhere any record of the fulfillment of the promised "Woe" connected with it. Surely the lightnings, voices, thunderings, earthquake, and hail connected with the opening of the heavenly temple (11:19) are not described like a "Woe" (cf. Rev 8:13—9:12; 9:12-21; 11:14-19), but rather as precursing signs of coming judgment. The portrait painted by the biblical narration is that the "Woe" on the seventh trump consists of the opening of the heavenly temple and the subsequent exodus from it of the seven angels with the bowls of wrath.

Thus, upon initial examination of the scriptural record, the chronological pattern of the unloosing of the judgments seems to be one of three successive series. The impact of seeing the heavenly wrath unfolded in this manner has been aptly put into words by Scott who has said,

> Now in the interval between these two [between the rapture and the second advent], the septenary series of judgment under the Seals, the Trumpets, and the Vials run their course. These divine chastisements increase in severity as we pass from one series to another. The judgments are not contemporaneous but successive. The Trumpets succeed the Seals, and the Vials follow the Trumpets. Strict chronological sequence is observed.... The Seals were opened in order that the successive parts of God's revelation of the future might be disclosed, but to faith only—the mass would regard the judgments as merely providential.[34] Such things had happened before. But the Trumpets' loud blast by angels intimates a public dealing with men of an intensely judicial character. These mystic Trumpets sound an alarm throughout the length and breadth of apostate Christendom. The public intervention of God in the guilty and apostate scene is thus intimated. Then in the third general symbol, that of the Vials or bowls poured out, the concentrated wrath of God overwhelms the whole prophetic scene under heaven. Chapter 16 reveals a series of judgments hitherto unsurpassed in range and severity.[35]

See Table 7 which follows for a visual representation of this succession pattern among the three heptads of divine castigation.

[34]Scott here uses the word "providential" in the loose sense, meaning "fatalistic." When this word, "providential," is used in other places throughout this study by the writer its stricter denotation is intended, God's holy, wise, and all embracing governing of the world through the agency of secondary causes.
[35]Walter Scott, *Exposition of the Revelation,* pp. 167-68.

Table 7

The Chronological Pattern of
the Unloosing of the Judgments

First seal (Antichrist)
Second seal (war)
Third seal (famine)
Fourth seal (death takes ¼ of the earth)
Fifth seal (martyrdom)
Sixth seal (heavenly & earthly disturbances)
Seventh seal

    First trumpet (earth ⅓ smitten)
    Second trumpet (sea ⅓ smitten)
    Third trumpet (rivers ⅓ smitten)
    Fourth trumpet (sun, moon, & stars ⅓ smitten)
    Fifth trumpet (locusts torment men for 5 months)
    Sixth trumpet (200,000,000 horsemen slay ⅓ of men)
    Seventh trumpet

heavenly temple opened

    First bowl (sores upon worshipers of the Beast)
    Second bowl (sea smitten entirely)
    Third bowl (rivers smitten)
    Fourth bowl (sun scorches men)
    Fifth bowl (darkness upon kingdom of the Beast; sores give pain)
    Sixth bowl (Euphrates dried to prepare the way of the kings of the East)
    Seventh bowl (exceeding great earthquake and hail; Babylon remembered for destruction)

When once it is seen that the scriptural account does indeed portray the judgments[36] as falling in three successive series, it becomes evident that the case for their actual chronological succession must be maintained even if at the present time human investigations cannot discover the divine method of bringing to pass every detail of this program. Thus, realizing that until that day dawns we will not be able to cement every detail in place, as God will surely then do, let us examine additional arguments for the succession of the three series, and the opinions to the contrary, being ever attentive to the weight of biblical evidence.

ADDITIONAL ARGUMENTS FAVORING SUCCESSION

The Missing Contents of the Seventh Seal and Seventh Trumpet

The seventh seal. Although some of the details of this argument are noted in the section immediately above in connection with the *prima facie* impression of the account,[37] it must here be specifically pointed out as an argument in its own right that if the seven trumpets are not contained in the seventh seal and if the seven bowls are not contained in the seventh trumpet, then the scriptural record gives no declaration of the contents of either. Note that the account of the effects of the sixth seal ends with the final verse of the sixth chapter of Revelation, chapter seven contains two parenthetical insets, and then chapter eight begins as follows,

> And when he opened the seventh seal, there followed a silence in heaven about the space of half an hour. And I saw the seven angels that stand before God; and there were given unto them seven trumpets (Rev 8:1-2).

From this point on the trumpets are dealt with and the seals are never again even mentioned. This is seen to be manifestly out of place (unless the seven trumpets be the contents of the final seal) when one considers that in Nestle's text of the Greek New Testament the space devoted to the description of each seal progressively increases as follows:

First seal	Revelation 6:1-2	5.5 lines
Second seal	Revelation 6:3-4	5.5 lines

[36]The *duration* of the several judgments has already been discussed; see chapter 4, part B.
[37]Chapter 4, part C.

Third seal	Revelation 6:5-6	7.1 lines
Fourth seal	Revelation 6:7-8	7.5 lines
Fifth seal	Revelation 6:9-11	10.7 lines
Sixth seal	Revelation 6:12-17	16.5 lines[38]

According to this progression the last seal should be treated in more detail than any of the previous ones, but instead (if the trumpets are not the content of this seal) only the 1.6 lines of Revelation 8:1, quoted above, are devoted to describing it in the Greek text even though when it was opened the sight was so awesome that a half hour of silence ensued (Rev 8:1).[39] Is this the silence of the end of the Tribulation or of the "end of the world?" There is not a hint in Scripture that this is so for as soon as Revelation 8:1 mentions the silence, Revelation 8:2, the very next verse, sees the fearful trumpets being given to the seven angels who are about to sound them. If the trumpets are not the content of the last seal, where are its missing contents?[40]

The seventh trumpet. It has already been said that unless the seventh trumpet be seen to contain the opening of the heavenly temple and the subsequent exit from it of the seven angels bearing the seven bowls, then the Apocalypse nowhere recounts the content of the seventh trumpet which is the third awful "Woe."[41] After a relatively brief treatment of the effects of the first four trumpet blasts (Rev 8:7-12), both the fifth and sixth soundings, the first two "Woes" (Rev 8:13; 9:12), are described to such an extent that in Nestle's Greek text over an entire page is taken up by the fifth and a complete page is the length of the sixth (Rev 9).[42] Since the seventh trumpet is also called a "Woe" (Rev 11:14-15) one would expect it also to be given an elaborate description. This is especially true when it is noticed that its opening is heralded by the greatest of promises, "But in the days of the voice of the seventh angel, when he is about to sound, then is finished the mystery of God" (Rev 10:7),[43] and is followed by wonderful reac-

[38]Eberhard Nestle; Erwin Nestle; and Kurt Aland, *Novum Testamentum Graece,* pp. 623-25.

[39]Ibid.

[40]See the lacuna in Lenski's commentary on Revelation on the verse dealing with the seventh seal, Revelation 8:1. After denying that the seven trumpets proceed from this seal, he does not give any positive explanation of what it may contain.

[41]See chapter 4, part C.

[42]Nestle, et al., pp. 629-31.

[43]The significance of this verse will be dealt with later in this chapter.

tions around the throne—heavenly voices are heard and the twenty-four elders fall on their faces in worship glorifying God with great declarations of praise to Him whose "wrath is come" (Rev 11:14-18). In addition to these awe inspiring actions there are "lightnings and voices and thunderings and an earthquake and great hail" when the heavenly temple is opened at the sounding of the seventh horn (Rev 11:19). Surely the sacred account could not just forget about the contents of the seventh trumpet, for when even the unheralded seven thunders are commanded to be sealed up there is notification given to the reader (Rev 10:3-4). Yet agreement is almost universal that the material of Revelation 12 which follows the sounding of the seventh trumpet at the end of Revelation 11 is parenthetical and not any part of the seventh trumpet at all. Lenski, as well as the others who oppose the view that the three series of judgments are successive, admits this.[44] Neither are the effects of the last of these trumpets found in the next chapter, Revelation 13, for that chapter shows the evil Beast triumphant in his greatest hour. If the content of the seventh horn is not seen in the opening of the heavenly temple and in the bowl angels which come from it, then in no place in the Apocalypse *does Scripture connect* the blast of the seventh trumpet with any record of what this blast achieves. Obviously its achievements have to do with the end of the pre-kingdom order (cf. Rev 11:15-18), but how then can the bowls be eliminated when it is through them that the Beast, the Antichrist,[45] and his kingdom are visited directly with divine wrath (Rev 16:2, 10)? The answer to this dilemma can only be that the seven bowls of wrath are the awesome contents of the seventh trumpet.

The Increasing Severity Among the Series

The fact that the judgments become progressively more severe as they move from the seals to the trumpets to the bowls weighs heavily in favor of the view that the three series occur successively rather than synchronously. This is true because while it is fitting and just for judgment to increase in harshness as impenitance increases during the Tribulation span, reason questions any theory that sees the same objects visited with wrath near simulta-

[44]R. C. H. Lenski, *The Interpretation of St. John's Revelation*, p. 361.
[45]The Beast of the Apocalypse, as a person, is the Antichrist. See chapter 1.

neously in *varying* measures of sternness. The point is, you may hit a child who remains recalcitrant three times, increasing the stroke's severity at each new display of rebellion—but who would strike a child, if it be possible, at the same time with three blows of differing intensity? If the severest of the three strokes is called for, there is no reason for giving two more moderate ones at the same time. The more moderate ones would be overshadowed and to no avail if a harder blow is given. Thus, in considering the possibility that the several series might be simultaneously unloosed, one quickly apprehends that it is not sensible to see the second trumpet smiting one-third of the sea at the same general time that the second bowl smites the sea (Rev 8:8-9; 16:3). Since the second bowl kills all life in the sea, "and every living soul died" even that which was in the sea (16:3), this must come after the second trumpet, which causes only one-third of all sea creatures to perish (Rev 8:9). Likewise, it cannot be believed that, as the third trumpet smites one-third of the rivers, the third bowl smites all the rivers completely (Rev 8:10-11; 16:4-7). Without a doubt the third bowl must come after the third trumpet. Likewise, when the fourth trump is partially *darkening* the sun (Rev 8:12), the fourth bowl cannot be at the same time *greatly increasing the sun's heat* (Rev 16:8-9). With respect to the sixth trumpet and sixth bowl, Buswell writes,

> Whereas at the sixth trumpet the river Euphrates is the place of the "loosing" of the four military powers [angels] and the outbreak of war, at the sixth vial (Revelation 16:12ff) the river Euphrates is dried up, to prepare the way of the kings from the East, who join the forces of the Beast at Armageddon, for the battle of the Beast against Christ (Revelation 19:17-21; cf. also vv. 11-16 and Revelation 20:1-3). All the factors harmonize with the greatest simplicity if the events of the sixth trumpet are taken as preceding those of the sixth vial by an interval of some time.[46]

Even if one here questions Buswell's taking of the four angels of Revelation 9:14 as military powers, or leaders of such, it is yet an undeniable fact that at the time of the sixth trumpet the Euphrates is still labeled as "the great river Euphrates" (Rev 9:14) and there is no hint of any change in this status, while at the sixth vial it is "dried up" (Rev 16:12).

From the above it is clearly perceived that the trumpets and

[46]Buswell, 2:432.

bowls cannot be synchronous, and that the line of evidence confirms the successive view concerning the three series of Tribulation judgments.

McClain, arguing for the successive view, points out the clear difference in severity among the three series when he says,

> The profound difference in these judgments is found in the degree of increasing severity as the several series run their course. Nothing could be more impressive than the contrast between what happens under the first seal and what happens under the last vial. The former releases an unnamed rider on a white horse who goes forth conquering and to conquer (6:1-2). The latter brings complete destruction upon the total world empire which he builds (chs. 17-18) and the doom of the conqueror himself (19:11-21). Between the beginning of the judgment period and its end, the storm of divine wrath falls upon the world with ever increasing intensity. For example, the first four seals bring judgment in events which are familiar to all men—war, famine, death. But the first four trumpets being *extraordinary* events, clearly supernatural in character: yet thus far affecting only a third part of its objects. When the first four vials are poured out, however, the supernatural judgments are no longer partial but become *universal* in their effects upon the inhabitants of the earth.[47]

Hoyt, a lifelong student of the Apocalypse, has concluded that the seals are "providential" in character, the trumpets are "semi-providential," and the bowls are "direct" supernatural visitations.[48] This observation of their progressive intensity also harmonizes with the symbols which represent each series. Seals (sing. *sphragis*) when they are broken, *reveal* and *release* the awesome contents which they have heretofore kept hidden. Trumpets (sing. *salpingx*) when blown *summon to battle* the host of an army; and when heard by the enemy, they serve to *warn* of the impending fray. Bowls of the wrath of God (*phialai tou thumou tou theou;* cf. Rev 16:1), at their pouring out, *cause a great quantity of stored up and concentrated wrath to fall* upon the heads of the impenitent. Thus these divine representations do not fit in

---

[47]McClain, p. 457. McClain notes that the 144,000 of Revelation 7:3-8 and the woman of 12:13-17, "both representing certain members of the nation of Israel," are the sole exceptions to those affected by the worldwide judgments.

[48]Hoyt, "Apocalypse," p. 124.

their symbolism three, or even two, simultaneously running sets of judgments; but rather, they better portray three sets of afflictions, each more intense than its predecessor. The seals *reveal* and *release* the previously hidden judgments upon a wicked generation; as the impious become more hardened the trumpets *summon to battle* God's armies and *warn* the sinners to repent; and finally, when the unrighteous are fully confirmed in their transgression, the bowls of the wrath of God are poured out *causing a great quantity of stored up and concentrated wrath to fall* upon the heads of the lawless ones who rebel against God and follow Satan.

Everything points only to an increasing severity from the seals, to the trumpets, to the bowls, and this progressive increase of severity in turn forcibly necessitates a temporal succession in the unloosing of the three series.

The Bowls Are Last; the Seals Are First

There is evidence to demonstrate adequately that the bowls are let loose after the seals and trumpets, and that they are specifically released near the end of the Tribulation. Likewise, the seals are seen as having their starting point at the start of the Tribulation period.

The bowls and the Beast. Since the bowls of Revelation 16 destroy the Beast's (Antichrist's) kingdom which flourishes during the last 3½ years of the Tribulation period (Rev 13:5)[49] the bowls must come at or very near the end of this seven year period. The following explanation shows this to be so.

While the descriptions of the seal and trumpet visitations do not contain as much as even one allusion to the Beast and his kingdom, the account of the bowls of wrath makes these the primary target for their onslaughts. The first bowl causes a grievous sore to come upon all that have the mark of the Beast on them and who worship his image (Rev 16:2). The fifth bowl is poured out directly upon the throne of the Beast causing his kingdom to be filled with darkness (Rev 16:10-11). When the sixth bowl is spilled the river Euphrates is dried to make way for the Eastern armies to come westward, and the mouth of the Beast, as well as that of the Dragon and the False Prophet, is used to entice the kings of all nations, to gather them together to the war of the great

[49]See chapter 1.

day of God Almighty (Rev 16:12-16).[50] Then finally, the seventh bowl completes the destruction of the Beast's world empire (Rev 16:17-21).[51]

Since the evidence has been shown to favor a relatively rapid pouring out of the bowls,[52] and since they (1) attack the Beast starting at the first bowl when men already have his mark upon them and are worshiping his image[53] and (2) culminate in the final three bowls when his kingdom is directly struck and destroyed (Rev 16:10-21), it must be concluded that the pouring out of these takes place during the era of the Beast's power—the final 3½ years of the Tribulation, and even in the latter portion of this period. Thus while the *terminus a quo*, or starting point, of these judgments cannot be placed more accurately at present than at some time after the middle of the week when the Beast arrives at his majority, the *terminus ad quem* or ending point, is definitely very near to Christ's appearance at the end of the Tribulation (Rev 19:19-20).

The seventh bowl, although extremely near the end of the Tribulation period, is not at its final end. This is seen to be true once it is recognized that the destruction of the city of Babylon described in Revelation 18 is accomplished at least in part by the seventh bowl. Thus in the account of the seventh bowl it is written,

> And the great city was divided into three parts, and the cities of the nations fell: *and Babylon the great was remembered in the sight of God*, to give unto her the cup of the wine of the fierceness of his wrath (Rev 16:19).[54]

Likewise, speaking of the city's judgment, Revelation 18:5 declares, "For her sins have reached even unto heaven, and *God hath remembered her* iniquities."[55] This latter verse in its context shows that God's remembering the city in the seventh bowl was identical to His destroying her in Revelation 18. Even the relative

[50]Author's translation.

[51]See the quotation of McClain cited on p. 103.

[52]See chapter 4, part B.

[53]The grievous sore "came ... upon ... the ones who were worshiping his [the Beast's] image" (Rev 16:2). Here "the ones who were worshiping" (*tous pros-kunountas*) is a *present* participle which follows an aorist verb, hence the translation, "were". The present (durative) tense here shows that the worshiping was continually going on at the very time that the first bowl was being emptied.

[54]Italics added.

[55]Italics added.

rapidity of the seventh bowl's destruction is confirmed in the remarks of Revelation 18 which cites the fall of the city as having taken place in "one day" or in "one hour" (Rev 18:8, 10, 17, 19). With this in mind, on the description of the seventh bowl in Revelation 16 Hoyt notes,

> The description of judgment in verses 18-21 *does not mark the absolute end.* It is quite evident from chapter 18 that men remain to bewail the destruction of the city of Babylon, and the events of chapter 19:11-21 must take place.[56]

The seven bowls are called the seven last plagues in Revelation 15:1. Alford, who asserts his own independence and want of any set system when it comes to interpreting each individual verse of the Revelation,[57] comments on the significance of this expression and on the chronological location of the bowls as follows:

> In the description, ch. xv. 1, which first introduces these plagues, they are plainly called *tas hepta plēgas tas eschatas* ["the seven plagues the last-ones"]. There can then be no doubt here, not only that the series reaches on to the time of the end, but that the whole of it is to be placed close to the same time.
>
> ....
>
> It [the bowl series] belongs, by its very conditions, exclusively to the time of, or to days approaching very near to the time of, the end.[58]

On the final expression in the same verse, Revelation 15:1, "for in them is completed *(etelesthē)* the wrath of God,"[59] Alford also remarks,

> It is to be observed ... that the whole of God's wrath in *final judgment* is not exhausted by these vials, but only the whole of His wrath in sending plagues on the earth *previous to* the judgment. After these there are no more plagues; they are concluded with the destruction of Babylon. Then the Lord Himself appears, ch. xix.[60]

J. B. Smith makes a potent observation concerning the chronological location of the bowls when he comments on the words, "Behold, I come quickly" (KJV), which appear in the letter to the Philadelphia church in Revelation 3:11. He says,

[56]Herman A. Hoyt, *The Glory: An Exposition of the Book of the Revelation,* p. 58.
[57]Alford, 4:248-49.
[58]Alford, 4:696-97.
[59]Author's translation.
[60]Alford, 4:693.

It is noteworthy that neither this [the expression, "Behold, I come quickly"] nor any other note of imminence pertaining to the second coming of Christ occurs in the entire tribulation section (chapters 6-18) until after the pouring out of the sixth vial (16:15) and just preceding the mention of Armageddon (16:16). From this we learn that *"Behold, I come quickly"* is the appropriate watchword for the church: "Behold, I come as a thief," for the tribulation saints. 16:15. In this connection compare I Thess. 5:4: "But ye, brethren, are not in darkness, that that day should overtake you as a thief."[61]

The fact that there is no note of the imminence of Christ's coming appearing amid the seal or trumpet accounts, not even amid the descriptions of the sixth or seventh judgments, while an admonition of imminence does appear between the sixth and seventh bowls, perfectly harmonizes with the position that the seals and trumpets chronologically precede the bowls, and that only the bowls are poured out close to the end of the Tribulation period.

The *terminus a quo* of the seals is by universal confession admittedly at the start of the period in view, futurists rightly seeing this to be at the beginning of the Tribulation. Furthermore the lone rider on the white horse of the first seal (Rev 6:2) has been shown to be the Antichrist just beginning his seven year journey of conquest.[62] Added to this is the amazing correspondence which the first five seals bear to Matthew 24:4-9.[63] The general belief of expositors who recognize Matthew 24-25 to be dealing primarily with the Tribulation is that *at least* the events of Matthew 24:4-7 (false christ, wars, famines, and pestilences) deal with the first 3½ years, for all of these happenings are specifically referred to in Matthew 24:8 as the "beginning of sorrows." On the basis of this the first four seals (Antichrist, war, famine, and death) are certainly to be likewise placed in these initial 3½ years.

If Matthew 24:9 also is still treating the first 3½ years, as Kent[64] and many students of prophecy aver, then since Matthew 24:9 deals with martyrdom and corresponds to the fifth seal, the fifth seal must also be unreservedly placed within the first 3½ year span. Favoring this is the fact that,

[61]Smith, p. 89.
[62]See chapter 4, part B.
[63]See chapter 4, part B.
[64]Kent, pp. 971-72.

The slaughter of the saints referred to at the opening of the fifth seal (Revelation 6:9ff) is explicitly said to be *not* the final time of Christian martyrdom (v. 11).[65]

That is, Revelation 6:11 says, "and it was said to them that they should rest yet for a short time, until also the number of their fellow servants and their brethren who are about to be killed as even they were should be completed."[66]

Thus, the martyrdom contemplated in the fifth seal not only need not correspond to that period of most intense persecution which takes place in the second 3½ years, but it assuredly must lie before it. Clearly, then, at this stage in the study it may be concluded that the evidence calls for at least the first five seals as a *minimum* occurring during the initial half of Daniel's seventieth week.

Conclusion. Evidence has been presented above to show clearly that out of the seals *at least* the first five occur in the first half of the week, while the bowls are poured forth entirely during the second half of the week, having their *terminus ad quem* near the very end of the week right before Christ's coming at His revelation (Rev 19). Thus it must be concluded that the seals and the bowls cannot possibly be thought of as being synchronous (the first seal is essentially the same item as the first bowl, only they are differently described, second seal and second bowl, etc.) or as being synchronously released (the first seal is let loose at the same moment as the first bowl, second with second). In fact, the beginnings of the first four seals *as a minimum* have been seen not even to be contemporaneous with any of the bowls. These facts make untenable the theory that the seals, trumpets, and bowls are contemporaneous.[67]

Part D
OBJECTIONS TO THE SUCCESSION VIEW

Objections already answered in previous discussions concerning the various approaches to the Revelation (preterit, historical, topical, futuristic—chap. 1) or concerning the presentation of the succession view (chap. 4 up to this point) will not be repeated

---

[65]Buswell, 2:431.
[66]Author's translation.
[67]See Buswell, 2:430-34, for additional discussion in favor of the successive view.

here; rather only those of a serious nature that have not yet been thoroughly dealt with will be treated.

CONCERNING THE SIXTH SEAL

The claim against the succession view which has to do with the sixth seal is succinctly stated by Lenski, who holds to the topical view of interpreting Revelation. On Revelation 6:12-17, the sixth seal, he writes,

> For those who will study Matt. 24:29 and II Pet. 3:10, 12 little comment will be needed. Here we have one picture of the end. The figures used are simply figures. Quaking, sun, whole moon (i.e., full moon), heaven, stars, mountains and islands are to be understood literally. The dispute as to whether this cataclysm is to be dated before or after what the futurists call the Great Tribulation and what they call the Rapture is unimportant. Here we get only one glimpse of the end of the world.
>
> A most important point to be noted is that the sixth seal places us at the *end*. In succeeding visions we are again placed there. The visions are synchronous prophecy that reaches the end.... The sixth [seal] presents only the end, really only certain phenomena occurring at the end.[68]

Lenski argues that Seal 6 is at "the end"; but I have placed it in the midst of the Tribulation period *before* the trumpets, bowls, and the establishment of the millennial kingdom (Rev 19:11—20:4). The issues here pivot on the answer to the real question at issue which is, Are the events of the sixth seal (Rev 6:12-17) *identical* to the events pictured in either Matthew 24:29 or 2 Peter 3:10 as Lenski assumes?

> But the day of the Lord will come as a thief; in the which the heavens shall pass away with a great noise, and the elements shall be dissolved with fervent heat, and the earth and the works that are therein shall be burned up (2 Pet 3:10).

From the context, it is clear that Peter is dealing with the dissolution of the first heavens and earth and the coming of the new heavens and earth. Thus he goes on to say,

> The heavens being on fire shall be dissolved, and the elements shall

[68]Lenski, pp. 239-40.

109

melt with fervent heat. But, according to this promise, we look for new heavens and a new earth, wherein dwelleth righteousness (2 Pet 3:12-13).

The burning of the first heavens and earth clearly takes place, as it will be seen in the sixth chapter of this study, *after* the Millennium and *not* during the final phase of the Tribulation period. God does not make all things new (Rev 21:5) until *after* the thousand years, when sin is finally forever banished. Thus John does not see the new heavens and earth with its New Jerusalem descending until Revelation 21:1-2 when he declares,

> And I saw a new heaven and a new earth: for the first heaven and the first earth are passed away; and the sea is no more. And I saw the holy city, new Jerusalem, coming down out of heaven from God.

In contrast to this, the events of the sixth seal occur during the Tribulation period. While some who interpret the Revelation according to the topical approach might argue that the seventh seal does not occur within the period discussed in chapters 6-19, no one can place the sixth seal outside of it—and this period is the Tribulation.

One might ask, "Could the events of the sixth seal begin during the Tribulation and continue on after it through the Millennium so as to culminate in the final burning of the earth which takes place after the thousand years are past?" This question must receive a negative answer for a tribulational judgment of wrath (cf. Rev 6:17) can hardly be conceived of as continuing throughout the Millennium when Christ is the actual Lord of the earth ruling in righteousness and reigning in peace.

It must also be recalled that after Christ comes at the end of the Tribulation period, the scene is not that of the old world and its works burned up (cf. 2 Pet 3:10), but it is one in which the living nations, standing on the same earth, are judged concerning entrance into the Kingdom (Matt 25:31-46).

While arguments could be multiplied on this point, it has been made sufficiently evident that the sixth seal could not be describing the final burning of the old earth spoken of in 2 Peter 3:10. Only those who refuse to see the existence of a Tribulation period between this present church age and a coming Millennium become confused on this.

Before leaving this topic a word should be said about the expression, "the day of the Lord," used in 2 Peter 3:10 to include the burning of the present world. This term has such a broad prophetical latitude that its use in 2 Peter 3:10 does not serve to place the event spoken of in any exact chronological location. This must be done on the basis of other evidence, as was done above. On the basis of Zephaniah 1:14-18; Zechariah 14:1-4; 1 Thessalonians 5:2; and 2 Peter 3:10, Pentecost defines "the day of the Lord" as follows,

> It is thus concluded that the Day of the Lord is that extended period of time beginning with God's dealing with Israel after the rapture at the beginning of the tribulation period and extending through the second advent and the millennial age unto the creation of the new heavens and new earth after the millennium.[69]

In dealing with the objection that Matt 24:29-30 and the sixth seal both describe "the end" rather than events within the seven year Tribulation period, let us proceed step by step. The verses in question declare,

> But immediately after the tribulation of those days (Eutheōs de meta tēn thlipsin tōn hēmerōn ekeinōn) the sun shall be darkened, and the moon shall not give her light, and the stars shall fall from heaven, and the powers of the heavens shall be shaken: and then shall appear the sign of the Son of man in heaven: ... and they shall see the Son of man coming on the clouds of heaven with power and great glory (Matt 24:29-30).

First, the heavenly signs spoken of in Matthew 24:29, quoted above, and in the parallel Mark 13:24-26, are explicitly stated to occur "immediately *after* the tribulation of those days" (emphasis added).[70] Since there exist no textual problems with these words in either Matthew or Mark they stand unchallenged;[71] and no amount of argument may be allowed to reverse their clear-cut teaching that the signs spoken of *follow immediately after* the "tribulation of those days." In this case the words "immediately after the tribulation of those days" must mean directly after the Tribulation period because the tribulation (*thlipsis*) described prior to this verse (Matt 24:4-28) includes both halves of the week and does not cease until it is ended by Christ's personal coming in

[69]Pentecost, pp. 230-31.
[70]Mark 13:24: *Alla en ekeinas tais hēmerais meta tēn thlipsin ekeinēn ho hēlios.*
[71]Nestle, et al., pp. 66-67.

the clouds. In fact things grow progressively worse until Christ comes at the end (Rev 19:19; Matt 24:22). Thus Matthew 24:29-30 teaches that the sun and moon shall be darkened and stars shall fall directly *after* the period of God's pouring out His wrath upon the earth in judgment plagues but yet *before* the manifestation of Christ in the clouds. Since Revelation seems not to permit any real gap between the two events, the end of the Tribulation period and the appearing of Christ (cf. Rev 19:11-21), the height of these heavenly manifestations, signifying the end of the age and the impending presence of the Judge of all the universe, probably occurs in a brief but intensely startling time span—perhaps only minutes. Then Christ is suddenly seen in the clouds.

Second, Lenski and others who put the sixth seal at the end of the judgment period take the sixth seal, the sixth trumpet, and the sixth bowl to occur all at the same time. However, even they cannot possibly claim that the multitude of horsemen slaying one-third of men in the sixth trumpet (Rev 9:13-21) or the events surrounding the dying of the Euphrates in the sixth bowl (Rev 16:12-16) occur *after* the period in question, which has been seen to be the Tribulation.[72] Thus the sixth seal, even if it were parallel to the sixth trumpet and sixth bowl, could hardly be outside of the period. Therefore, even if the theory (which states that the sixth seal, sixth trumpet, and sixth bowl all occur at the same time) were taken as true for the sake of argument, the sixth seal must yet be seen as being opened *during* the Tribulation and not *after* it.

Third, in connection with Luke 21:25-27, a parallel or near parallel to Matthew 24:29-30, it must be noted that there are other heavenly signs reported in Revelation during the Tribulation period in addition to those of the sixth seal. Luke 21:25-27 reads,

> And there shall be signs in sun and moon and stars; and upon the earth distress of nations in anxiety because of the roaring and tossing of the sea; men fainting from fear and expectation of the things coming upon the inhabited world: For the powers of the heavens shall be shaken. And then they shall see the Son of Man coming in clouds with power and great glory.[73]

The verses make clear the fact that heavenly signs (*sēmeia*— plural) shall precede Christ's coming; however, they do not de-

---

[72]See Introduction and chapter 1 of this book.
[73]Author's translation.

clare when the signs will commence, how long they will last, nor whether the heavenly signs will continue uninterrupted once they begin or whether they shall be interspersed with time intervals between them.

When chapters 6-19 of the Revelation are examined it is discovered that heavenly signs besides those of the sixth seal are manifested quite frequently during the Tribulation era. Indeed both the trumpet and bowl series manifest heavenly signs with the cataclysms of the third trumpet (falling burning star), fourth trumpet (a third part of the sun, moon, and stars smitten with darkness), and fourth bowl (sun affected; scorches with intense heat) displaying *unquestionable* cases of the heavenly powers being affected, while other of the judgments no doubt also see the heavenly powers vacillate from their usual courses (hail and fire in the first trump, etc.). Beyond all doubt and cavil these do not represent one grand cosmic finale, but instead a series of disturbances in the heavenly sphere which are manifested periodically during the Tribulation period. This well fits the Lord's description in Luke 21:25-27 of heavenly signs occurring before His coming, although it by no means exhausts the description.

Fourth, it is to be carefully noted just what occurred when the sixth seal is opened. When it was set loose there was a great earthquake, the sun was blackened, the moon became blood red, stars (probably meteors and possibly numerous glowing, star-like, man-made satellites) fell, "the heaven was separated (apechōristhē) as a scroll which is rolled up," and every island and mountain was moved (Rev 6:12-14).

Of course, if the heavenly calamities of the sixth seal are predominately symbolical as Ironside claims rather than literal physical signs, then there is no problem at all and no need to reconcile this seal with Matthew 24:29-30. Ironside states,

> It is therefore not a world-wide, literal earthquake that the sixth seal introduces, but rather the destruction of the present order—political, social, and ecclesiastical—reduced to chaos; the breaking down of all authority, and the breaking up of all established and apparently permanent institutions.
>
> The sun, the source of light and life for this planet, speaks of supreme authority, and is the well-known type of the Lord Himself.... But soon He [Christ—the sun] will be entirely rejected and His

word utterly despised. Thus will the sun be blotted out from the heavens . . . Naturally enough this will mean the complete destruction of all derived authority, so we next read, "the moon became as blood," . . . The stars falling from the heaven indicate, I take it, the downfall and apostasy of great religious leaders, the bright lights in the ecclesiastical heavens. In Daniel, those who turn many to righteousness shine as the stars. In the first part of our book the stars are said to be the messengers of the churchs. So it would seem clear that we are to understand the symbol in the same sense here.[74]

However, there is a deep question as to whether or not such political, social, and ecclesiastical calamities could evoke the response from men that is shown after the sixth seal when they implore the rocks to fall on them so as to hide them from the wrath of God (Rev 6:15-17). Besides this, the events of the sixth seal, even though they are cast in the language of appearance, are described as literal physical occurrences and there is insufficient warrant to interpret them as social upheavals (cf. Psalm 46:2, 6).

In order to fathom what did and what did not happen in Matthew 24:29-30, we must heed the reaction on earth to these events. Men on earth of every class hide themselves in caves and in the rocks of the mountains: they implore the rocks to fall upon them to hide them from the face of God; and they declare that the great day of wrath has come (Rev 6:15-17). These reactions of men then on earth show that a world-destroying final explosion has not yet here occurred. Unless it is kept in mind that the language of appearance is used, the KJV translation of Revelation 6:14 can be misleading in its saying, "the heaven *departed* as a scroll," as can be the ASV which says, "the heaven was *removed* as a scroll."[75] Properly, "the heaven was *separated (apechōristhē)* as a scroll which is rolled up," is a more accurate rendering.[76] Compare this with Acts 15:39 where the same word *(apochōrizō)* is used to signify the *parting* of Paul and Barnabas.

What actually shall take place in that day may be difficult for us to conceive precisely since we have never experienced a parallel to it. Swete's explanatory conjecture is enlightening.

'Like a papyrus roll when it is being rolled up'; i.e., the expanse of

---

[74]Harry A. Ironside, *Lectures on the Book of Revelation*, pp. 114-17.
[75]Author's emphasis.
[76]Arndt, p. 101, defines *apochōrizō* as *separate*—in the passive, *be separated*. The expression of Revelation 6:14 is translated, *the sky was split*.

heaven (Heb., *harakea;* Gr., to *stereōma*) was seen to crack and part, the divided portions curling up and forming a roll on either hand. The conception is borrowed from Isa. xxxiv. 4.[77]

Arndt's "the sky was split" may even more correctly describe the *appearance* of that which will occur. Perhaps, since the sun is thoroughly blackened, the description may in the language of appearance describe such a rapid unparalleled blackening of the sky that the heavens themselves appear to have been rolled away.[78] In any case, what should be noticed is that the biblical account gives the undeniable impression that *during and after* the events of this seal, men on earth are still alive and caves, rocks, and mountains still exist (Rev 6:15-17). No description of multitudes dying is here given (cf. Rev 6:8; 8:11; 9:18; 11:13). Therefore any interpretation errs that sees these events as the end of the cosmos or the end of the earth. Likewise, since at the end of the Tribulation period an angel is seen standing in the sun, in the background of the sun, crying to the birds who fly in mid-heaven (Rev 19:17) it is seen that at the very end of the Tribulation the sun still exists as do birds and the atmosphere of the earth. In fact, at the very coming of Christ, John sees "the heaven opened" (Rev 19:11), and it is safe to say, there is no warrant for seeing in this sight a scene of the new heavens. When all of these things are considered together the evidence is seen to indicate that the effects of the sixth seal are primarily designed to fill the inhabitants of the earth with terror rather than to kill them off or end the world. This effect most fittingly follows the slaying of many martyrs which occurs after the fifth seal is opened.

On the nature of the sixth seal, Buswell remarks,

> I conjecture that the cosmic disturbances of the sixth are to be taken both literally and figuratively. They are certainly given in emphatic form. Perhaps we of the late twentieth century are just about to enter the time of these disturbances. It may be that the upheavals in nature which John pictures symbolize atomic warfare. Whatever the detailed meaning, great disaster is certainly signified.[79]

Fifth, another reason for not seeing the heavens as completely done away with by the sixth seal and for not identifying it as being identical with the heavenly signs that shall occur *immediately*

---

[77]Swete, p. 93.
[78]Arndt, p. 101.
[79]Buswell, 2:436.

before Christ comes in the clouds is as follows: If, as almost all acknowledge and as this study has already demonstrated, the trumpets are more grievous than the seals, the last three of them being especially severe and being called "Woes" (Rev 8:13; 9:12; 11:14); and the bowls are likewise more intense than the trumpets, being called the last plagues (Rev 15:1);[80] that interpretation that makes a seal, the sixth, more fearsome than most of the trumpets and bowls must be inaccurate.

Sixth, if the sixth seal is opened soon after the fifth, as is probably the case, and if the sixth seal were that final cataclysm before the Lord's coming to judge the nations on earth (Rev 19:11-21), the words of the fifth seal predicting further martyrdom could hardly have sufficient time to come to pass.

Seventh, it is to be noted that the cry of earthly men upon seeing the effects of the sixth seal, "for the great day of their wrath is come" (Rev 6:16-17), does not prove that this seal is identical to the astral signs which Matthew 24:29-30 shows taking place immediately *after* the Tribulation. This is because (1) the sentiment of the men is natural in the face of such circumstances,[81] and (2) the entire Tribulation is seen as a time when God's wrath is poured out, especially during the spilling of the *bowls of wrath* (Rev 15:1; 16:1), and therefore this term, "the great day of their wrath is come," cannot be merely confined to the judgment of the nations after the Tribulation (Matt 25:31-46) nor to even the judgment of the great white throne (Rev 20:11-15).

Conclusion. From the lengthy discussion above, it must be concluded that the events of the sixth seal occur *during* the Tribulation and are recounted in the language of appearance, in the way that they look to an ordinary spectator, rather than in the precise terminology of modern day astronomy, cosmology, or geophysics. The evidence weighs against identifying these happenings, either with the final fiery consummation spoken of by Peter (2 Pet 3:10) or with the astral phenomena, occurring immediately *after* the Tribulation, that accompanies the return of the Lord in the clouds (Isa 12:9-10; Joel 3:15; Matt 24:29-30; Mark 13:24-26). Thus the chronologist is not forced to place the opening of the sixth seal at

[80]See chapter 4, part C.

[81]When shooting stars fell for three hours during the evening of November 13, 1833, terrified people thought that the end of the world was upon them (Clarence Larkin, *The Book of Revelation*, p. 61).

the very end of the seven years—which would leave no room for the trumpets and bowls to follow in time and would thereby eliminate the successive view.

On these heavenly disturbances, Buswell gives the following excellent conclusion:

> Isaiah 34:4 is quoted in part in Christ's Olivet discourse. (Mt. 24:29; Mk. 13:25; Lk. 21:26), Christ there refers to the stars falling from heaven, which, if a literal prediction, can only mean a shower of meteors.
>
> Instead of Isaiah's word in regard to the heavens being "rolled together as a scroll," Christ refers to "the powers of the heavens being shaken." But Christ does not contemplate the removal of the present heavens and earth in these words, for He continues and says that at that time we will see the Son of Man coming in the clouds of heaven, and the elect will be gathered from the remote places of the earth.
>
> In Revelation 6:13, 14, at the opening of the sixth seal, John refers to the stars falling from heaven and also includes Isaiah's reference to the heavens departing as a scroll when it is rolled up. John's following words, however, made it clear that he does not mean that the sidereal universe is removed or ceases to exist, for he describes events on earth as continuing one after another. We know very well that biblical writers distinguish the cloudy heavens from the starry heavens, and "the third heaven" (2 Cor 12:2) is the spiritual heaven. If the references to the heavens departing as a scroll being rolled up are to be taken literally (and I think they are) then they must surely refer to terrific storms and rolling clouds. I well remember a certain stormy aeroplane trip in which I saw a great black cloud with rolling edges which resembled the rolled edges of a scroll. Isaiah 34:4 certainly does not contemplate anything remotely resembling the removal of the heavens and the earth which Peter and John describe [2 Pet 3:10-13; Rev 21:1-5], nor does Christ in the Olivet discourse or John in his description of the events of the opening of the sixth seal describe any such event.[82]

As Newell says, the sixth seal is

> The *first* darkening of the sun and moon, "before the great and terrible day of the Lord" (Acts 2:20 quoting Joel 2:31). The *second* will be "immediately after the tribulation" (Matthew 24:29). But

---

[82]Buswell, 2:529.

men in terror believe the end has come! When it does not, they grow hardened like Pharaoh, and we see them in Revelation 19:19 boldly gather to war against the Lamb whom here they dread![83]

CONCERNING THE SEVENTH TRUMPET

It may be objected against the view which sees the three series of judgments as successive that the words of the angel in Revelation 10:6-7 indicate that the seventh trumpet is blown at the very end of the Tribulation, and that therefore there is insufficient time allowed to the series of bowls to follow *after* it. Revelation 10:6 says,

> And he [the angel] swore ... that there shall be time no longer, but in the days of the voice of the seventh angel, when he is about to blow, even the mystery of God shall be completed as He gave the good tidings to His servants the prophets.[84]

To answer this objection that pivots around the difficult passage quoted above, all that is necessary is that an interpretation be shown to be plausible which permits the series of bowls to come out of the seventh trumpet. Pursuant to this let it first be noted that the words "there shall be time no longer" (*hoti chronos ouketi estai;* Rev 10:6) must mean that "there shall be delay no longer," and so the ASV translates it. Hoyt well says,

> The substance of his [the angel's] message is—"delay no longer." This does not mean that time comes to an end. For time had a beginning [when God created the universe] but will never have an end. Verse 7 explains the meaning. It here has reference to time in the sense of delay in the execution of a plan. (Cf. Matt. 24:40ff.) "My Lord delayeth his ..." chronīzeī mou ho kurīos).[85]

On the mystery that was to be "completed" Hoyt adds,

> This mystery is to be finished at the sounding of the seventh trumpet.... This mystery was why a God of holiness and power allowed evil to go on unpunished and good to suffer. Why does God not establish his kingdom and rule over men? Hab. 1:2-4; Psa. 73. When Christ came and was rejected, the mystery became deeper.... The proof that this general interpretation is correct is recorded in 11:15-19. [Rev. 11:15-18—"And the seventh angel sounded; and

---

[83]Newell, p. 108.
[84]Author's translation.
[85]Hoyt, *The Glory*, p. 134.

there followed great voices in heaven, and they said, The kingdom of the world is become the kingdom of our Lord, and of his Christ: and he shall reign for ever and ever.... We give thee thanks, O Lord God,... because thou hast taken thy great power, and didst reign. And the nations were wroth, and thy wrath came,... to destroy them that destroy the earth."][86]

Consistent with the above understandings, the successive interpretation (seals first, trumpets next, bowls last) sees the blowing of the seventh trumpet as the further initiation of God's forceful suppression of evil *by means of* the pouring out of the bowls of wrath at the seventh trumpet's blast. This is the explanation of Revelation 10:6's cry that at the blowing of the seventh trump there would be "delay no longer." Thus Revelation 10:6 by no means must be taken to prove that the seventh trump is blown at the very end of the seven year Tribulation.

The sayings of the voices at the blowing of the seventh trumpet, "The kingdom of the world is become the kingdom of our Lord" (Rev 11:15-18) are *proleptic*, like many prophecies of old, Isaiah 53, in absolute confidence of their certainty they treat as present or past things which have not yet fully occurred.[87]

Consistent with this explanation is the following set of facts which center about the heavenly temple: (1) at the sounding of the seventh trumpet the *heavenly temple* is seen *opened* (Rev 11:15, 19); (2) after the intervening inset episodes of Revelation 12-14 are shown, the sequence is continued again with the sight of the opened *heavenly temple* and the seven bowl angels coming out of it in order to pour out their seven portions of the wrath of God (Rev 15:5-6); and (3) *immediately after* the final bowl of wrath is spilled, a voice comes *out of the heavenly temple* saying, "It is done" (gegonen; Rev 16:17). This not only points to the seventh trumpet's containing the seven bowls (through the intermediary of the heavenly temple), but it also confirms the fact that that which was begun with the sounding of the seventh trumpet is accomplished at least in part through the agency of the series of bowls.

The above explanation not only is the only one that perfectly accords with the biblical picture surrounding the heavenly temple, but it also silences the objection here in question against the

[86]Ibid., p. 135.
[87]Smith, pp. 149, 157.

successive view of the seal, trumpet, and bowl judgments. It does this by providing a reasonable and plausible interpretation of the blowing of the seventh trumpet and the promises that go with it while yet allowing time after its initial sounding for the bowls to be poured out.

CONCERNING EARTHQUAKES AND THUNDERINGS

This objection is concisely summed up by Buswell. He writes,

> It has been alleged that the recurrence of such items as "voices and thunderings and lightnings and an earthquake" indicates that each of the series ends at the same point in chronology. These words occur three times, 8:5, 11:19; and 16:18-21, and in the last two "hail" is added to the list.[88]

So Jamieson, Fausset, and Brown's commentary, which sees the three sets of judgments as synchronous, remarks,

> Again, the *earthquake* that ensues on the opening of the sixth seal is one of the catchwords, i.e., a link connecting chronologically this sixth seal with the sixth trumpet (ch. 9:13; 11:13); cf. also the seventh vial, ch. 16:17, 18.[89]

As these phenomena are examined it is apparent that the "lightnings and voices and thunders" symbolize God's presence *coming nigh* for judgment. Thus they are seen at the giving of the Law at Sinai (Exod 19:16ff) and at the Throne of Adjudication in heaven (Rev 4:5).[90] Earthquakes and hail have the same significance in the Apocalypse but they also bring with them great physical violence and disaster (Rev 11:13; 16:18-21).

The occurrences of earthquakes, thunders, and other things are shown on Table 8, which follows.

Upon surveying this chart and the biblical account it is seen that although an earthquake appears in the sixth seal, none can be found in either the sixth trumpet or bowl. Jamieson, Fausset, and Brown's remark, which is quoted above, claims to connect the quake of the sixth seal with one in the sixth trumpet and gives Revelation 9:13 and 11:13 as the supporting references. This is

---

[88]Buswell, 2:432-33. Buswell, it should be made clear, does not subscribe to this objection.

[89]Jamieson et al., p. 1525.

[90]The title for the throne is from Newell, pp. 85-86.

certainly in error for though Revelation 9:13 tells of the blowing of the sixth trumpet (no earthquake) and 11:13 speaks of an earthquake, it is a rare interpreter indeed, no matter what the school, who considers the earthquake of Revelation 11:13 to be within the sixth trumpet. The sixth trumpet clearly ends at Revelation 9:21 and the next verse, 10:1 begins with the words, "And I saw," and then goes on to narrate a new vision—that of the "sun-faced angel and the little book" (Rev 10:1-11).[91] This is followed by another vision, that of "Israel, the two witnesses, and the Beast" (Rev 11:1-13). Both of these visions are "inset"[92] parenthetical explanatory "episodes,"[93] and are clearly differentiated by their subject matter from the contents of any of the seal, trumpet, or bowl judgments. After these two visions have been exhibited, *then* the series of trumpets is resumed with announcement that the seventh one is coming quickly since the sixth one has already been blown (Rev 11:14-15). However, it is in the midst of the second parenthetical vision that the earthquake of Revelation 11:13 is seen, and not in connection with the sixth trump as Jamieson, Fausset, and Brown's comment mistakenly states. The quake of Revelation 11:13 marks the ascension of God's two witnesses and the seven thousand killed during it is God's judgment on the wicked people who approved of the slaying of His two faithful servants; it has nothing whatsoever to do with the two hundred million horsemen of the sixth trump (Rev 9:13-21)!

Why also Jamieson, Fausset, and Brown wish to connect chronologically the sixth seal, sixth trumpet, and the *seventh* bowl is a query which offers an interesting insight. For if the judgments are synchronous the sixth item of each series and the seventh of each series should be the ones that match.[94] However, there is also a similarity between the expressions, "And every mountain and island was moved out of its place" (Rev 6:14; sixth seal) and "Every island fled away, and the mountains were not found" (Rev 16:20; seventh bowl). Yet since the sixth seal and the seventh bowl have a "great earthquake" (Rev 6:12; 16:18) in common, it is not strange that a similar expression is used to describe the far reaching effects of each. Again it must be said, similar

---

[91]Hoyt, *The Glory*, p. iii.
[92]Ibid., pp. iii, 117, this is Hoyt's title for such visions.
[93]This is J. B. Smith's title for such visions. Smith, p. 149.
[94]Jamieson et al., p. 125.

descriptions do not prove identity—especially here during a period of "earthquakes in divers places" (Matt 24:7).

In view of this,

> We must conclude that the mention of such phenomena gives no ground whatever for synchronizing the series, no more than the earthquake at the crucifixion (Matthew 27:51f.) can be synchronized with the earthquake at the resurrection (Matthew 28:2).[95]

Table 8
Thunders, Voices, Lightnings, Earthquakes, and Hail as Found in Revelation 4-19

Reference	Event	Description
4:5	Lightnings, voices, and thunders	At the throne scene; these *precede the seals.*
6:12	A great earthquake	One of the disturbances of the sixth seal.
8:5	Thunders, voices, lightnings, and an earthquake	These *precede the trumpets.*
10:3-4	Thunders	The seven mysterious thunders.
11:13	A great earthquake	7000 killed; an accompaniment of the raising of the two witnesses.
11:19	Lightnings, voices, thunders, earthquake, and great hail	Follows the blowing of the seventh trumpet and the sight of the opened heavenly temple; these *precede the bowls.*
16:18-21	Lightnings, voices, thunders, a great earthquake, and exceeding great hail	Follows the pouring of the seventh bowl and the voice from the heavenly temple, saying, "It is done"; the earthquake and hail cause worldwide destruction.

[95]Buswell, 2:433.

The question has been examined as to whether the seals, trumpets, and bowls were three successive series or three synchronous contemporaneous series. It has been seen that the *prima facie* impression of the biblical account points to the successive view that the seals come first, the seventh seal yields the trumpets, and that in turn the seventh trumpet yields the heavenly temple out of which comes the seven final bowls of wrath. This scheme, upon closer study, was seen to stand.

Other arguments were also seen to have favored the successive view. It was found that the synchronous theory (that the three series all happen at the same time) left the contents of both the last seal and the last trumpet unexpectedly unexplained. It was also noted that the increasing severity among the series progressing from the seals to the trumpets to th bowls could only fit harmoniously with their successive arrangement. It was realized at this time that the second trumpet had to precede in time the second bowl and that the third trumpet likewise had to precede the third bowl, and that certainly these trumpet and bowl series not only were not different descriptions of the same events, but that they also were not even different events occurring at the same time.

It was next discovered that the opening of seals began at the start of the seven year Tribulation, with at least the first five seals being placed in the initial 3½ years. The bowls, however, were assuredly to be located in the second 3½ years of the Tribulation week, starting probably late in that span and ending very near to the close of the seven years.

When the major objections to the successive view were studied it was found that neither the loosing of the sixth seal nor the initial sounding of the seventh trumpet could be placed at the close of the Tribulation. It was then specifically observed that events of the sixth seal were not identical with the heavenly signs which immediately precede Christ's coming at the close of the seven years (Matt 24:29-30) nor with that great and final fiery consummation spoken of in 2 Peter 3:10. The claim was looked into that such signs as thunderings and earthquakes when correlated prove the synchronism of the three series. This allegation, after study, was set aside as untrue.

Along with the above, in Buswell's words, "Attention should also be given to the total absence of any positive evidence of the alleged synchronization."[96] When these many factors are placed together, the conclusion can only be that the theory that the three sets of judgments are contemporaneous must be labeled as untenable; and the view that the three sets are successive in the order of seals, trumpets, and bowls must be adjudged as completely sustained. Thus, Larkin must be confessed as correct when he writes concerning the seventh seal the following:

> We must not forget that the "SEVENTH SEAL" includes all that happens during the sounding of the "Trumpets," and the pouring out of the "Vials," and so extends down to the ushering in of the Millennium. To illustrate, a rocket fired into the air may burst into "seven stars," and one of these stars into "seven other stars," and one of the second group of stars into a third group of "seven stars." So the "Seventh" Seal includes the "Seven Trumpets," and the "Seventh" Trumpet includes the "Seven Vials."[97]

It was also noted in part B that within each set of seals, trumpets, and bowls the several judgments will also be released in successive order. Once, however, the various judgments were sent forth their outworkings and effects were discovered to continue in time for various durations while other subsequent judgments were being released. In this sense, and in this sense alone, the judgments become contemporaneous.

Thus in response to the major inquiry of this chapter it can now be said that the judgments are not only successive within each series, but that among the three series themselves there is succession—from the seals to the trumpets to the bowls.[98]

[96]Ibid., 2:434.

[97]Larkin, p. 68.

[98]On the question as to how far the judgments have progressed when the midpoint of the seven years is reached the following may be noted:
(a.) The middle of the seven years marks the point when the Antichrist, the Beast, commits the abomination of desolation, declares himself publicly to be a god (Dan 9:27; Matt 24:15; 2 Thess 2:3-4), assumes the position of world dictator (Rev 13:4-8), and launches his persecution against Israel and the saints (Dan 7:25; Rev 13:5-7).
(b.) It has been shown above in part C of this chapter that as a minimum at least the first five seals must be set loose upon the world during the first half of the week and that the bowls occur in the last half of the week near its end. Thus the

judgment being released by the midpoint could be either the sixth or seventh seal (placing the trumpets entirely in the last 3½ years) or one of the trumpets. If the seventh trumpet blows at the midpoint of the week then the six trumpet judgments of Revelation 8 and 9 would all take place during the first 3½ years.

(c.) Scholars are divided on this question. Pentecost (pp. 362-63) spreads the trumpets through the second 3½ years and puts the bowls at the very end prior to Christ's appearance of Revelation 19. Yet he does this by making the trumpet judgments to chiefly represent the troop movements of end-time armies in opposition to their literal heavenly-plague significances. This type of interpretation seems here to be questionable on hermeneutical grounds.

(d.) Buswell (2:450-60), Hoyt (The Glory, pp. 40-44), Larkin (pp. 80-89), J. B. Smith (pp. 149-61), and others hear the seventh trump at the midpoint placing the trumpet devastations in the former half of the seven years. Arguments to favor this are: ((1)) The parallel between Daniel 10:5, 6; 12:6, 7 and Revelation 10:1-7. Here it is urged that where the angelic speaker in Daniel 12:6-7 claims that the Great Tribulation will be finished in 3½ more years, the same angelic speaker in Revelation 10:5-7 in a parallel moment says that the seventh trump will sound. Hence the seventh trump sounds when 3½ years of the seven remain—at the midpoint of the week! (See Smith, pp. 149-61 on this complex argument). ((2)) It is urged that at the blowing of the seventh trump the Ark of the Covenant appears (Rev 11:19) which signifies that "Jewish things" are now in view. Since God will save Israel out of her prophesied tribulation, called "the time of Jacob's trouble" (Jer 30:7) during the last 3½ years of the week (Dan 7:25; 9:27; Matt 24:15-22; Rev 12:6, 14), it is argued that the showing of that sacred golden box at the blowing of this trumpet shows that the exact midpoint of the week has at last arrived for then God will remember His covenant with Israel of which the Ark of the Covenant is a symbol. ((3)) Some who believe that the rapture will occur in the middle of the seven years identify the rapture trumpet of 1 Corinthians 15:52, "the last trump," with the seventh trumpet of Revelation. See the final footnote at the close of chapter 3 that is contrary to this idea. ((4)) The trumpets (Rev 8-9) nowhere speak of the kingdom of the Beast as do the bowls (Rev 16) and thus may occur in the first half of the week before the Beast, the Antichrist, comes into his world power in the final 3½ years (Rev 13:5; Dan 9:27).

(e.) There are other arguments, replies, and counter arguments for the above views. Walvoord (The Revelation of Jesus Christ, p. 123), places even the seals along with the trumps and bowls in the last half of the week. But I have already shown, in chapter 4, part C, why I believe definitely that at least the first five seals at the minimum belong in the first 3½ years.

(f.) While the original chapter 5 of my dissertation concluded that the seventh trump's beginning marked the midpoint of the heptad of years, I have now modified my conclusion on the matter. I have not been fully convinced by any of the arguments given on this issue nor has my personal study yielded a sure answer. My inclination is at present that the Lord wishes to focus our eyes on the middle of the week's commission of the abomination of desolation (Matt 24:15-22; 2 Thess 2:3-4; Dan 9:27) and He does not wish us to get our eyes off of this main feature of that hour by our being diverted upon a consideration of which particular judgment may happen at that time to be in progress.

The first seal begins the seven years and the first five at least occur in the former 3½ years; the seven bowls come rapidly in the final 3½ years near its end; and the seven trumps blow between the seals and bowls! (See chapter 4, parts C and E.) Since God, in the book of Revelation, does not appear to me to have attempted to reveal which particular judgment is in progress at the week's center—be it the sixth seal, the seventh, the fourth or last regular trumpet, or the fifth or first "Woe" trumpet (cf. Rev 8:13; 9:12; 11:14), or the great final seventh trumpet of Revelation 11:15-19—I will here let the matter go with my opinion that it must be somewhere at the beginning, middle, or end of the seven trumpet plagues. The compass needle swings to and fro and it has not yet stopped, yet its direction is toward the trumpets.

5
Revelation 6-19:
The Chronological Placing of the Insets

After the major chronological positioning of the seals, trumpets, and bowls has been determined, as is the case in the study at hand, it is at once noticed that the happenings of the Tribulation, Revelation 6-19, have by no means yet been exhausted. This is so because, amid and after the narrations of the three judgment series, there lies a body of material located in Revelation chapters 7, 10-14, and 17-19 which contain various additional explanatory and supplementary sequences. These are accounts, often parenthetical in nature, inserted just at the right moment as "insets" or "episodes" so as to give a clearer total picture of past, present, and future happenings.[1]

Thus in the midst of the unremitting continuous judgments of the seals and trumpets in chapters 6, 8, and 9, chapter 7 is inserted as an "inset" to show the mercy and salvation of God taking place during this era. Then before the reader comes to the awful bowl judgments of chapters 15-16, lest he wince at their severity or be dull of understanding, the insets of chapters 10-14 give him a vision of the total picture. They enable him to see the worldwide empire of the Antichrist which daily grows more powerful, more blatantly wicked, and more defiant of God. At last, after the bowls have been seen to be emptied of their wrathful contents in Revelation 16, chapters 17-19 are inset to display the details of the final righteous destruction of the earthly kingdom of evil, which is consummated with the coming of Christ at the finale of the period (Rev 19:11-21).

---

[1]On the propriety of the insets see, William Kelly, *Lectures on the Book of Revelation*, pp. 150-52.

127

Utilizing the findings made thus far, the time has now come to examine each of the insets individually so as to determine their chronological bounds; whether the events or descriptions within each concerns the entire Tribulation week, the first half of the week only, the second half only, or whether its borders transcend the limits of the Tribulation so as either to flash back into the distant past or to lunge into the post-tribulational future. In the case of each inset vision, the attempt will be made to fix its overall general position in relation to the eschatological program of God. A complete exegesis of each vision or the temporal identification of every verse in the several insets, if only for spatial reasons, is, of course, beyond the scope of the present study. It must also be kept in mind that the examination of each inset is built on the entire prior study up to that point, for only this fact can justify the brief treatment given to certain points that have been previously established.

THE 144,000 SEALED (REV 7:1-8)

Here in the midst of the terrible seal and trumpet devastations is seen the first of two inset visions which show that God is gracious in mercy even in an hour of judgment. The question to be here investigated is, When does this sealing of the 144,000 take place?

Before answering the question asked above, several things should be noted. This sealing evidently marks the ones sealed as those owned by Christ—thus His mark is placed upon their foreheads and its wearers are immune from His judgments (Rev 7:1-3; 9:4). Antichrist, in like manner, attempts his own counterfeit of God's sealing by forcing his subjects to accept his diabolical mark upon their foreheads or right hands (Rev 13:16-18).

The ones sealed are physically of the seed of Israel. This is shown by the Spirit, explicitly making it plain that twelve thousand out of each of the Israelite tribes are to be so marked (Rev 7:4-8). The symbolic nature of the numbers twelve thousand and 144,000 (cf. Rev 21:12-17) need not eliminate their literal significance. Only those amillennialists and British Israelite proponents who reject the scriptural teaching that God has yet a future glorious program for Israel will attempt to put aside the clear words of this vision. In that lamentably oft repeated manner, while leaving Israel with all of her ancient curses, they proceed to give all of her promised future blessings to the church or to some other body.[2]

The sealing chronologically must take place sometime in the earlier portion of the Tribulation. In Revelation 9:4, in the description of the fifth trumpet, the infernal locusts are given authority to torment, "only such men as have not the seal of God on their foreheads." Thus it is clear that the sealing will have been completed before the start of the fifth trumpet, and consequently, before the seven bowls which fall in the later portion of the week.

The command to the four angels in Revelation 7:3 enables the time of the sealing to be even more accurately set. This command orders,

> Injure not the earth, nor the sea, nor the trees, until we have sealed the servants of our God upon their foreheads (Rev 7:3).[3]

The "earth," "sea," and "trees" are the three items specifically forbidden to be attacked "until" (achri) the sealing is finished. When the initial trumpets are inspected, it is seen that in the first two, a third part of the earth and a third part of the trees are burnt with fire, while the third part of the sea becomes blood (Rev 8:7, 8).[4] Thus, since the seals do not especially affect either sea or trees, it is safe to conclude that the command given in Revelation 7:3 was given just prior to the blowing of the first or second trumpets.

Whether these Jews will accept Christ as their Messiah and Saviour at the time of their sealing, before it, or after it may be debated, but it is certain that they will know and love Him as their Lord before a long time shall elapse. Since they are called "the servants of ... God" (Rev 7:3) it is not out of place to recognize these as Christ's own end-time heralds of the "gospel of the kingdom" that is to be preached in all the world before the end comes (Matt 24:14).

Much more could be said concerning the wonder of these doings, but according to the task at hand, the primary target has

[2]See Introduction.
[3]Author's translation.
[4]The KJV here omits the words, "a third part of the earth was burnt up" (Cf. ASV). They are in the oldest Greek manuscripts, Eberhard Nestle; Erwin Nestle; and Kurt Aland, *Novum Testamentum Graece*, Revelation 8:7.

already been struck; it has been observed that the sealing of Revelation 7:1-8 will take place in the first half of the seven years sometime prior to the blowing of the first trump. It will possibly occur after the seals, but since the fifth seal is "martyrdom," the 144,000 may well be sealed even before this time.

THE GREAT MULTITUDE (REV 7:9-17)

This inset shows an innumerable throng clothed in white robes, which have been washed "in the blood of the Lamb," standing before the throne and the Lamb. Thus, the reader of the Apocalypse, between learning of the seal judgments on the one hand and learning of the fearful realities of the trumpets, bowls, and the persecution of the Beast on the other, can constantly be assured of the fact that, through all the turmoil of the period, God will yet save an immense throng out of every nation, tribe, people, and tongue (Rev 7:9).

Let it be noted that concerning this multitude it is said, "These are the ones coming out of the great tribulation" (Rev 7:14).[5] The Greek text contains the definite article before the words "great tribulation" *(tēs thlipseōs tēs megalēs)* in Revelation 7:14.[6] It is therefore a certainty that "the great tribulation" referred to here is identical with the one "great tribulation" *(thlipsis megalē)* which Jesus foretold would come immediately following the occurrence of the abomination of desolation (Matt 24:21). Thus Hoyt writes,

> It [the Greek expression, "the great tribulation"] makes this period a specific time, namely, the last three and one-half years when Antichrist will turn all of his hatred against the people of God (Jer. 30:7; Dan. 12:1; Matt. 24:21-22).[7]

This redeemed throng will stand about the throne in the very presence of the four living creatures, the twenty-four elders, and the angels (Rev 7:9-11). Their days of hungering and thirsting are forever over, and they serve the Lamb both night and day (Rev 7:15-16). From this description this multitude appears to be in the realm of *"the blessed dead in heaven."*[8] Therefore Newell boldly and correctly asserts,

[5]Author's translation.
[6]Nestle et al., Revelation 7:14.
[7]Herman A. Hoyt, *The Glory: An Exposition of the Book of Revelation*, p.33.
[8]J. Oliver Buswell, Jr., *A Systematic Theology of the Christian Religion*, 2:438-40.

I would rather credit the general spirit of reverent commentators of all the Christian centuries (which regards this company as a heavenly one) than the opinions of some, whose awakened sense of the literalness and glory of the millennial kingdom led them, in commenting on both chapter 7 and 21:9, to ascribe to earthly millennial times what the passages themselves necessarily make heavenly and eternal.[9]

When it is considered (1) that Hitler's persecution annihilated six million Jews during the six year era of the Second World War in Europe, September 1, 1939 to May 8, 1945; and (2) that the persecution of the Antichrist against the godly during the Great Tribulation will be a more fearful deluge than that of Hitler's (cf. Matt 24:21); the literalness of John's narration of the innumerable multitude can be understood. These include the martyrs of this period, men and women of every tribe and tongue who, refusing to obey the Antichrist, die in martyrdom for Him who had already died for them.

Considering that the world's population is over four billion and still growing, it is easily seen that a "great multitude which no man could number"[10] (Rev 7:9) could possibly all be martyred during the Tribulation period. A second part of the throng can remain alive through persecution, while still being faithful to Christ and so gain admittance to the millennial Kingdom (Matt 25:31-46). And the majority of the earth's population can still be left to follow the Antichrist to destruction (Matt 25:31-46; Rev 13, 17, 18, 19). Thus the view that the great multitude of Revelation 7:9-17 pictures the Tribulation saints, many or all of whom will be martyred during the final 3½ years, is seen not only to be a biblical one, but it also is observed to be one that is feasible with today's rising population figures.

In concluding, let the following observation be noted. In Revelation 6:11 those to be martyred in the last half of the week are specifically called the "fellowservants" and "brethren" of those seen under the altar in the fifth seal (Rev 6:9-11) who were slain during the first half of the week. This, combined with the fact that in Revelation 20:4 all of the martyrs of the Tribulation period are seen as one company, argues strongly for the proposition that the martyrs of the first half of the week are also included with those of

---

[9]William R. Newell, The Book of The Revelation, p. 115.
[10]An immense number, though not an infinite one.

the last half in this immense throng out of all nations in Revelation 7:9-17.[11] This is especially true since those who so perish in the former half of the week are in a real sense the wavesheaf of the harvest that will follow in Satan's great hour during the final 3½ years of the Tribulation.

THE ANGEL AND THE LITTLE BOOK (REV 10:1-11)

The appearance of the sunfaced angel to John, the conversation between the two, and John's eating of the little book, of course, were happenings that took place c. A.D. 95-96 after John had experienced, in the spirit, the work of the sixth trumpet angel but before the seventh had sounded (cf. Rev 9:12-21; 11:14ff.). These events, such as John's eating the book, will not again occur *as such* during the actual future Tribulation period, but are descriptive of those things which will be bitter and sweet during the blowing of the seventh trumpet (Rev 10:6-11).

Concerning the substance or chronology of the "seven thunders," one must observe that they are mentioned only briefly in Rev 10:3-4, with the immediate admonition, "Seal up those things which the seven thunders uttered, and write them not." It may be said with J. B. Smith, "It is folly for anyone to venture a guess as to the content of the words of the seven thunders."[12] Newell's words are also apropos:

> It is characteristic of that presumption which belongs to error that Seventh Day Adventism professes to tell us ... the very things which the seven thunders uttered: although God commanded John to seal them up and write them not [Rev. 10:3-4].[13]

THE TWO WITNESSES (REV 11:1-13)

There are two primary items of chronological concern which must be examined in this inset, and they are both spoken of in Revelation 11:2-3 which says,

> And the outer court of the sanctuary leave outside and measure it not, for it is given to the gentiles, and the holy city they shall tread under foot forty and two months. And I shall give to my two wit-

[11]This line of argument was suggested by Dr. James L. Boyer, Grace Theological Seminary.
[12]Jacob B. Smith, *A Revelation of Jesus Christ*, p. 155.
[13]Newell, p. 142.

nesses, and they shall prophesy a thousand two hundred sixty days clothed in sackcloth.[14]

The Measuring of the Temple

In Revelation 11:2 it is declared that the Gentiles are to tread down "the holy city" for forty-two months or 3½ years. This obviously points to a period of Gentile domination over the earthly city of Jerusalem. The question is, When will this period occur? The answer is not hard to find. This is true because it is clear that: (1) during the first half of the week some sort of a protective covenant will be in force between Antichrist and Israel (Dan 9:27; cf. Isa 28:15, 18) and (2) from the abomination of desolation which occurs at the middle of the week unto the end, Antichrist will be in complete control and he will be persecuting Israel and the saints everywhere, especially those in Judaea (Dan 9:27; Matt 24:15-22). Now it stands to reason that if the Jews are being persecuted by Antichrist and his *worldwide* (hence Gentile) force (Rev 13:7-8) in *Judaea*, at this time Gentiles must be "treading under foot" Jerusalem and its environs. Thus the statement of Revelation 11:2 connected with the measuring of the Temple can only be interpreted so as to signify that final period of Gentile mastery over Israel which will occur in the last 3½ years of the Tribulation immediately before Christ comes to rescue His own.

The Ministry of the Two Witnesses

Revelation 11:3-13 describes the powerful ministry of the two men who are witnesses of God in a hostile world.[15] Verse 3, quoted above, says that God shall give "power" [understood, though not in the Greek text] to His two witnesses so that they may prophesy for 1,260 days, or 3½ years. Again, here the chronological issue to be settled is, When do these 3½ years occur?

In pursuit of this answer it is to be noted that for 1,260 days the witnesses prophesy, and during this time they cannot be harmed

---

[14]Author's translation. "Gentiles" refers to non-Jewish nations.

[15]See Hendriksen who allegorically takes the two witnesses to be "the church militant." W. Hendriksen, *More Than Conquerors: An Interpretation of the Book of Revelation*, p. 155. When did the church militant have the power to stop the heavens from raining (Rev 13:6)?

(vv. 3-6). Then, "when they shall have finished their testimony," the Beast, who is the Antichrist,[16] shall kill them in Jerusalem and not permit their bodies to be buried for 3½ days, (vv. 7-9).[17] After these 3½ days, during which time the earth dwellers rejoice over the death of the witnesses, God shall resurrect His two witnesses and take their bodies into heaven.[18] At that time there shall be an earthquake in Jerusalem that will kill seven thousand (vv. 10-13).

With this information it is seen that the ministry of the two witnesses must be placed in the initial 3½ year span for the following reasons:

First, at the end of the second 3½ year period the Beast's followers are lamenting over Babylon's doom and are gathering for the great battle at Armageddon, and finally slain by Christ, whose coming is surrounded with the powers of the heavens being shaken (Rev 16-18; 19:11-21; Matt 24:29-30). This picture does not harmonize well with the 3½ days of rejoicing and gift giving in which the earth dwellers participate following the murder of the witnesses (Rev 8:10). This discordance between the end of the second 3½ year period and the 3½ days, *following the end* of the 3½ year ministry of the witnesses, makes it most unlikely that the prophesying of God's two servants takes place during the latter half of the week.[19]

Second, if their ministry occurs in the former half of the week and ends exactly at its middle, then the murder of the two witnesses takes place at the same time as the abomination of desolation when the Beast proclaims himself as the god of this world (2 Thess 2:3-4). Whether he slays the two witnesses and then commits the abomination, or if he commits the abomination and then proceeds to kill the witnesses; in either case, the picture corresponds to his then initiating his persecution of Israel from that time onward while he enjoys an almost unhindered domination of the earth (Matt 24:15-22; Rev 13:4-8). All fits together if the witnesses fulfill their term during the first 3½ years.

[16]See chapter 1.

[17]The killing, resurrection, and earthquake all take place "in ... the city ... where their Lord was crucified" (Rev 11:8), Jerusalem.

[18]It was earlier stated at the close of chapter 3, immediately prior to the conclusion of that chapter, that the command to John in 4:1 to "Come up hither" did not prove the doctrine of a pretribulational rapture. In like manner it must be here said with equal vigor that the same command, "come up hither," given in 11:12 to the two witnesses in the middle of the week does not prove a midtribulation rapture.

[19]See Table 4.

Third, it is possible that *if* it were God's will for the two witnesses to speak *openly* against the Beast during his time of murderous persecution and worldwide unhindered power during the latter half of the week, they could at the same time remain alive for 3½ years while doing this. It is, however, a much more reasonable view to see the *irrepressible* two witnesses empowered by God for their ministry during the first half of the week, slain in the middle after they have run their course, and then to behold the *irresistible* Beast in power during the second half of the week (Rev 11:3-7 cf. 13:4-8).

Fourth, in light of the explicit dichotomy by which Daniel's seventieth week is divided into two equal halves, and the confirmation of their exact equality in length by various references in the Apocalypse (Dan 9:27; Rev 11:2-3; 12:6, 14; 13:5),[20] the thought cannot be entertained that the 3½ year ministry of the two witnesses, so explicitly set forth as 1,260 days (Rev 11:3), might cross the middle of the week without corresponding to either the first or the second clearly marked divisions.

In light of these strong arguments, it must be unhesitatingly concluded that the ministry of the two witnesses, who are clothed in sackcloth, corresponds to the first 3½ years, that they are slain by the Beast at the midpoint of the week, at the time he commits the abomination of desolation, and that tme 3½ days they lie dead are the first days of the second half of the week. Thus, it is realized that the forty-two months of Revelation 11:2 tell of the iniquitous Gentile dominion of the last 3½ years, and the 1,260 days of Revelation 11:3 speak of God's messengers to the world during the first 3½ years.[21] In these two verses, Revelation 11:2-3, the entire course of Daniel's seventieth week is therefore comprehended (Dan 9:27).[22]

On the power and effects of the message of the witnesses during the first 3½ years of the Tribulation, Hoyt remarks,

[20]Ibid.

[21]Clarence Larkin, *The Book of Revelation,* p. 84, assigns the two witnesses to the last half of the week simply because (1) the prior statement of Rev 11:2 concerning the treading down of Jerusalem refers to the last 3½ years, and because (2) this prior statement speaks of forty-two months which is the same length as the 1,260 day ministry of the two witnesses. This forgets that the first half of the week is also 1,260 days long, and that merely because one item follows another they cannot automatically be regarded as dealing with the same time period (e.g., Matt 4:16-21 cf. Isa 61:1-2).

[22]Hoyt, *The Glory,* p. 41.

The importance of their testimony cannot be overestimated (Rev. 11:4).... By their testimony, it is my opinion, they bring about the conversion of the 144,000 who will become the witnesses during the final half of the tribulation period.[23]

THE WOMAN AND THE DRAGON (REV 12)

The Characters

The identification of the basic characters of this important inset is essential before the chronological problems can be successfully solved. The woman is seen as the first "great sign" in Revelation 12:1. She is clothed with the sun, the moon is under her feet, and she wears a crown of twelve stars. Genesis 37:9-11, Joseph's dream, pictures the dormant nation Israel, composed of Jacob, who is "Israel," his wife (Rachel, who was Joseph's mother), and his twelve children as a sun, moon, and twelve stars—Joseph himself being the twelfth star. From this, the identification of the woman in this inset as representing the nation Israel is beyond all cavil. Also the subsequent description of the persecution of the woman for 3½ years (Rev 12:13-17), perfectly fits Antichrist's 3½ year persecution of Israel.[24]

This conclusion is further corroborated by Revelation 12:5 which says of the woman,

> And she was delivered of a son, a man child, who is to rule all the nations with a rod of iron: and her child was caught up unto God, and unto his throne.

Here the man-child who came from Israel is Christ ("for the salvation is out of the Jews"—John 4:22;[25] Mic 5:2-3; and Rom 9:5 which plainly declares that Christ came from the nation Israel after the flesh). It is He whom Psalm 2:7-9 declares will rule the nations "with a rod of iron." The words, "her child was caught up to God, and unto his throne," refer to Christ in the same manner as does the Apostles' Creed when it says, "He ascended into heaven and sitteth on the right hand of God the Father Almighty."

However, the final confirmation of the woman's being Israel is a comparison of Revelation 12:7-9 with Daniel 12:1-7. In Revelation

---

[23]Ibid., p. 42.
[24]See chapter 1.
[25]This is said by Christ to the woman at the well of Sychar. Author's translation.

12, we see a woman being persecuted by Satan, and Michael the archangel at this time fights against Satan (vv. 7-9). Likewise, in Daniel 12:1 when Daniel's people are said to be in their "time of trouble such as never was since there was a nation," a time lasting 3½ years (3½ times—Dan 12:7), Michael "shall ... stand up" and contend for Israel, Daniel's people. Thus both Revelation 12 and Daniel 12 show Michael contending against Satan concerning the 3½ year Great Tribulation of Israel. The matter is settled, (1) Genesis 37:9-10 shows the woman to be Israel; (2) Romans 9:5 says that Christ came from Israel, so the woman of Revelation 12 must also be her; and (3) Daniel 12:1-7 shows that it is the nation Israel, the remnant, for whom Michael fights in the final Great Tribulation and hence here, in Revelation 12:7-9 when he is fighting Satan who wishes to persecute the woman, we must conclude that she is Israel.

Seiss, who, from his pages on this topic, never seems to have had Genesis 37:9-11 with its sun, moon, and stars representing the young nation Israel called to his attention, has a different outlook.[26] He identifies the woman as the "visible church" and the man-child who comes out of her as the "invisible church."[27] Yet, as Kelly points out, "Israel was the mother of Christ," and the church is the "heavenly bride," the "Lamb's wife."[28] Without hesitation it can be said that "the sun-clothed woman represents Judaism and the nation Israel," and that her child represents Christ.[29]

Buswell suggests that the woman of Revelation 12 is identical to the apostate harlot church of Revelation 17:3 because the former flees into the "wilderness" (Rev 12:14) and the latter is also seen in "a ["the" in KJV] wilderness."[30] Buswell here sees the child not as Christ, but as the true church. However, this unusual conjecture disregards the plain evidence for the woman of Revelation 12 being Israel who bore the man-child Christ, and has *the harlot church giving birth to the true church.* This is so improper that it must be adjudged as an inadmissible view. One like factor cannot

[26]Joseph A. Seiss, *The Apocalypse,* 2:278-85; 2:295-303.
[27]Ibid., 2:297-98.
[28]Kelly, pp. 248-49.
[29]Hoyt, *The Glory,* p. 45. Also, see Pentecost, pp. 285-90, for a full discussion on the identity of this woman. After dealing with the several theories, he concludes. "The woman can be none other than Israel, with whom God has His covenants, and to whom those covenants will be fulfilled" (pp. 287, 290).
[30]Buswell, 2:479.

prove identity when other conflicts exist. Otherwise, Christ could also be taken to be identical with either the woman in Revelation 12 or the woman in Revelation 17 merely because He too spent time in the "wilderness" (Mark 1:12-13).

If the "wilderness" in both Revelation 12 and 17 represents the wild and chaotic surface of the earth with its masses in confusion then it is an apt picture in chapter 12 for Israel scattered and hiding throughout the globe, and it likewise well fits the harlot church of chapter 17 in terms of her presiding over worldwide religious confusion, barrenness, and desolation.

The other sign in the heavens was the "great red dragon" who had seven heads and ten horns (Rev 12:3). This is none other than Satan, the Devil, as the text plainly declares (Rev 12:9). Michael (Rev 12:7-11), of course, is the archangel (Dan 10:13, 21; 12:1; Jude 9). With these identifications established, the chronological issues may now be undertaken.

The Time of Revelation 12:1-5

Revelation 12:1-5 quite plainly reaches back far prior to the Tribulation period. They contain allusions to ancient Israel's "travailing in birth" to bring forth the Messiah; Satan's causing one third of the angels to fall with himself (v. 4); Satan's attempt to kill the Christ child at His birth through Herod (v. 4; Matt 2); and to the ascension of Christ forty days after his resurrection (v. 5). Thus this portion of the inset vision speaks of "Israel's conflict with the Dragon in the past."[31]

The Time of Revelation 12:6, 13-17

After the position of Revelation 12:6, 13-17 is determined, then verses 7-12 may be returned to and correctly assigned.

The two time indications in these verses are contained in verses 6, 13-14, which read as follows:

> And the woman fled into the wilderness, where she hath a place prepared of God, that there they may nourish her a thousand two hundred and threescore days.... And when the dragon saw that he was cast down to the earth, he persecuted the woman that brought

[31]Herman A. Hoyt, "Apocalypse," pp. 143-46.

forth the man child. And there were given to the woman the two wings of the great eagle, *that she might fly into the wilderness* unto her place, *where she is nourished for a time, and times, and half a time,* from the face of the serpent.[32]

It is obvious that verses 6 and 13-14 convey essentially the same story. In both cases the woman, Israel, is fleeing from a satanic persecution against her, and she is nourished and protected by God for 3½ years. Both the 1,260 days of verse 6, and the three and one-half "times" of verse 14 have already been seen to unquestionably equal 3½ years.[33]

Now when the Scriptures are searched to determine when and where Satan has ever or shall ever persecute Israel for a period of this length, it is found that at one time, and at one time only are these specifications met, namely, when Antichrist persecutes Israel during the "Great Tribulation," the last 3½ years of Daniel's seventieth week (Jer 30:4-7; Dan 7:21, 25; 8:25; Matt 24:15-22).[34] During this time God "nourishes" and preserves many out of the Israeli nation for at its end "they shall look upon me [Christ] whom they have pierced" (Zech 12:10-11) and be converted as a nation. Possibly the "wilderness" refers to the host of Gentile humanity among whom the Jews are scattered (cf. Matt 25:31-46).

The credibility of this view is reinforced when it is considered that the Beast of the Apocalypse, who has been shown to be the Antichrist,[35] has "ten horns and seven heads" (Rev 13:1); while here in Revelation 12:3, the Dragon who is Satan is also seen to have "seven heads and ten horns." Thus, doubt is cast aside, for clearly *Satan is in the Antichrist* when the latter persecutes the nation Israel for the final 3½ years of the Tribulation period. To this persecution, the passage at hand refers, and therefore it can aptly be entitled, "Israel's conflict with the Dragon *in the future*."[36]

The suggestion of the historical school that this period refers to 1,260 *years* within this present church age, and the similar opinion of the topical school that it refers to the entire present age,

32Author's emphasis.
33See chapter 1.
34Ibid.
35Ibid.
36Hoyt, "Apocalypse," p. 147.

have both already been dismissed.[37] They have been seen to be the results of the *a priori* requirements of these systems.[38]

The Time of Revelation 12:7-12

These verses which show the war in heaven with Michael and his angels fighting Satan and his angels, already discussed above, are seen to be a parenthetical element occurring between verses 6 and 13. The duration of the war is not here divulged, and even the word translated "war" in Revelation 12:7 (*polemos*) does not give us a clue to the duration of the conflict for it can refer to "a single engagement" as well as to a lengthy war made up of numerous protracted battles.[39]

However, the end of the heavenly conflict is distinctly manifested in Revelation 12:13 which says,

> And when the dragon saw that he had been cast unto the earth, he persecuted the woman who had given birth to the man child.[40]

This shows that the Dragon persecuted the woman immediately upon his being cast from heaven to earth. Since in the discussion of Revelation 12:6, 13-17 just previous to this one it was seen that this particular persecution of the woman, Israel, begins at the midpoint of the Tribulation and continues for 3½ years throughout the last half week, it is an escapable conclusion that the ending point of the "war in heaven" is at the midpoint of the week, exactly coincident with the launching of the anti-Israel persecution.[41]

It can well be reflected in light of Revelation 12 that any person who finds himself holding anti-Semitic attitudes should ask himself whose side he is on—the side of God who will preserve Israel in the wilderness or on the side of the Dragon who hates the woman?

[37]See chapter 1.

[38]Ibid.

[39]William F. Arndt and F. Wilbur Gingrich, *A Greek English Lexicon of the New Testament and Other Early Christian Literature*, p. 691.

[40]Author's translation.

[41]Hoyt, "Apocalypse," p. 146, entitles this section, Rev 12:7-12, "Israel's conflict with the Dragon in the Heavens."

For an exhaustive treatment on this subject, see Thomas T. Julien, "The War in Heaven—Revelation 12:7-9." B.D. critical monograph.

Julien supports the view that this passage tells of a literal battle at the time of the second advent.

The central figure of this inset is the Beast who rises out of the sea (v. 1), who is the Antichrist.[42] Concerning the career of this Satan-inspired man much has already been seen to be revealed elsewhere in Scripture and in the Apocalypse.[43] In the chapter at hand, Revelation 13, many clarifying details are added to complete the portrait of this "man of sin ... the son of perdition" (2 Thess 2:3), and a chronological keystone is among these. This keystone is Revelation 13:5, and once it is set into place other conclusions can be supported by it. This verse, Revelation 13:5, says,

> And there was given unto him a mouth speaking great things and blasphemies, and there was given to him authority to continue forty and two months.[44]

The question is, To what time period do these forty-two months refer?

In placing these forty-two months into the eschatological calendar it is first noted that this period which equals exactly 3½ years must obviously refer to the time of the Antichrist's greatest power. Thus in verse 5, he is given forty-two months "to continue" (poiēsai), "to do" his will, "to proceed" with his plans and desires, "to accomplish" his wishes, "to make" things happen according to his own will.[45] All of these similar thrusts are contained in this verb poieō.[46] The implication is that this period sets God's limitation on the permitted reign of this "wild beast" (thērion—v.1), and that at the end of the 3½ years of "authority" (exousia) which he is granted in verse 5, his activities will be ended.

This forty-two months of the Antichrist's authority beyond all doubt must be assigned to the last half of the Tribulation period. The account of Revelation 13:4-8 tells that blasphemy, persecution of the saints, worldwide political and military power, and worldwide religious supremacy will be the characteristics of this time. This corresponds exactly to the description of this period

---

[42]See chapter 1.
[43]Ibid.
[44]Author's translation.
[45]Arndt, pp. 687-89.
[46]Ibid.

that is given in the rest of the Bible.[47] Persecution of God's people (Matt 24:15-22), blasphemy (Dan 7:25; Matt 24:15; 2 Thess 2:3-4), vast political and military might as shown by the power to conduct a persecution and subdue kings (Dan 7:19-25; 9:26; Matt 24:15-22), world religious leadership (Matt 24:15; 2 Thess 2:3, 4; Dan 7:25; 8:25), and these all within a duration of 3½ years (Dan 7:25; 9:27), give the picture of the Antichrist's season of power. This picture perfectly duplicates the one found in Revelation 13. This flawless harmony which arises from so many directions, like the evidence for a sound textual reading which comes from agreeing manuscripts originating out of the four quarters of the ancient world, proves the correctness of the above contention, that the forty-two months of the Beast's authority correspond to the last awful 3½ years of the Tribulation.

With the above keystone in place, the entire chronology of this inset may be constructed. Thus Revelation 13:4-18, the entire inset except for its initial three verses, is seen to speak of the Beast in his vicious day of power. During this season of 3½ years there will also be two additional characteristics concerning which these verses increase our knowledge.

First, a second personage called both the "Beast *out of the earth*" and the "false prophet" will arise out of *the earth* ("the land" of Palestine?), and he will cause the world to pay their supreme religious homage to the first Beast, the Antichrist, through the use of lying wonders (Rev 13:11-18; 19:20; cf. Matt 24:11).

Second, a system of worldwide commercial control will be instituted so that no one can do any buying or selling unless they have the mark of the blasphemous Beast on either their right hand or their forehead (Rev 13:16-18). This is the awful picture of the forty-two month season when the earth is ruled by the "Infernal Trinity," the Dragon, the Beast, and the False Prophet (Rev. 13:1, 4, 11, 14).

Revelation 13:1-3 sees the first Beast, the Antichrist, rise out of the sea, and it tells of the satanic imitation of the resurrection of Christ whereby the Antichrist, the final head of the Beast,[48] is

[47]See chapter 1, Table 2.

[48]For a thorough investigation of the identity of the Beast's seven heads see H. Keith Binkley, "Meaning of the Seven Heads in Revelation 17:9," B.D. critical monograph.

Binkley, pp. 46-49, concludes that the seven heads represent "seven kingdoms

killed, but manages somehow to live again ("and the wound of his death was healed,"—Rev 13:3, 14). The former of these two happenings, the Beast's rise out of the sea, verse 1, points to his origin from among the troubled nations represented by the vast sea (cf. Rev 17:15).[49] His rise is recounted as follows:

> And he stood upon the sand of the sea. And I saw a beast rising up out of the sea, having ten horns and seven heads, and upon his head names of blasphemy (Rev 13:1).[50]

If the seer is here taken to be standing at Patmos, then he is looking out upon the Mediterranean Sea. If this be the case then the Antichrist gradually "rising up" (anabainon—present participle having a durative force) from amid the nations surrounding the Mediterranean harmonizes perfectly with the other Scriptures that witness to his coming out of the Revived Roman Empire—the empire which encircled the Mediterranean (Dan 9:26; 7:19-23).

---

which have been influenced by paganism (false religion, religious harlotry) throughout the course of their history." He names these kingdoms as Egypt, Assyria, Babylon, Medo-Persia, Greece (these are the five which have "fallen"—Rev 17:10), Roman Empire (this is the head that "is"—Rev 17:10), and the Revived Roman Empire (this is the head yet to come which will only last a short while—Rev 17:10). The Beast "that was and is not" who is the eighth, but one of the seven (Rev 17:11), refers to the Antichrist and his kingdom in the last 3½ years of the Tribulation period. After his resuscitation in the middle of the week, he becomes dictator of the Revived Roman Empire, and he and his kingdom become the "eighth" who "is out of the seven," this is simply another aspect of the seventh head, the Revived Roman Empire (Rev 17:11; cf. 13:3).

Zahn, when speaking of the heads of the beast says, "Since Revelation was written at the time of the Roman Empire, this is, according to xvii. 10, the sixth head; another seventh kingdom will follow it, but will not long reign. Upon this follows the eighth,—that of the antichrist,—which, however, is only a revivication of one of the five earlier kingdoms. Without question this is intended to be the Graeco-Macedonian and its typical ruler, the pre-Christian antichrist, Antiochus Epiphanes.... The interpretation of the seven heads as the line of Roman emperors from Augustus or from Caesar onwards, which has confused many, is untenable." (Theodore Zahn, "The Writings of John." In Introduction to the New Testament, translated by M. W. Jacobus et al., 3:441-42).

Certainly the number of heads, seven, in company with the many sevens of the book of Revelation, exhibits the totality of that which is signified. Thus the seven heads symbolize the entire run of historic Babylon-type, satanically led pagan kings and empires. That final one, that of the Antichrist, "is the eighth, and is of the seven" (Rev 17:11). It is the last great culmination of the evil traits of the Babylonian kings and kingdoms which have previously dominated the world scene. It is the Satan-possessed Antichrist who as the final head of the beast leads the world in rebellion against God.

[49]Hoyt, "Apocalypse," p. 150.

[50]Author's translation.

This rise must be assigned as taking place in the first half of the Tribulation week for by its midpoint Antichrist already is at the height of power (Matt 24:15-22 cf. 2 Thess 2:3-4).

The resurrection of the Beast (as Christ!) so that "the whole world marveled after the Beast" (Rev 13:3, 14) must be the gigantic lever used of Satan to allow the Beast to declare himself to be a God and to cause the world to accept him as such (2 Thess 2:3, 4; Rev 13:4, 8, 12, 15). When the immensity of the act, by which a man proclaims himself to be this world's deity and is accepted as such by the unregenerate population of the globe (Rev 13:8), is considered, it is soon readily admitted that no ordinary set of even remarkable circumstances could accomplish so staggering a result. What is the explanation for this immense effect? It can only lie in an equally immense cause—the resuscitation of the Beast. With this in mind it cannot be far amiss to place the resurrection of the Beast shortly before his entering into the Temple to proclaim himself "God." That occurs at the midpoint of the week. With this final item assigned, this examination of the chronology of the inset of Revelation 13 is concluded.

THE 144,000 UPON ZION (REV 14:1-5)

> And I saw, and behold, the Lamb standing upon the mount Zion and with Him an hundred forty-four thousand having His name and the name of His Father written upon their foreheads (Rev 14:1).[51]

The questions to be answered concerning this inset are: Who are the 144,000? Where are they? and, When does this appearance take place? The identification of this group is necessary in order that the time of the event, the chronological factor, might have some significance.

Concerning the identity of this blessed company it must be said that this group is composed of the same 144,000 who were seen sealed in Revelation 7:1-8. On this assertion J. B. Smith's argument is conclusive. He writes,

> These hundred forty and four thousand are apparently the same company as those mentioned in 7:1-8. Were this not the case, it would be an exception to the usual careful distinction made by the sacred writer by the use of "another." For instance, note "another beast," "another angel," "another sign," "another voice"; hence we

[51]Author's translation.

should have here "another" 144,000. Observe too, that mention is made of a seal or mark of identification upon (Greek) *their foreheads* ["having His name and the name of His Father written upon their foreheads." Rev. 14:1.] Cf. 7:3 ["Saying, injure not the earth ... until we have sealed the servants of our God upon their foreheads"].[52]

That this group redeemed from among men is called "firstfruits unto God and unto the Lamb" (Rev 14:4) indicates that these were the first Israelites (for the company in Revelation 7:1-8 were Israelites) to look to Christ for salvation after the church was removed and the Tribulation commenced. It is only later at Christ's coming and during the Millennium that the full crop is harvested. At the Lord's appearance "they [Israel as a nation] shall [at last] look upon me [Christ] whom they have pierced" (Zech 12:10), and "all Israel shall be saved" (Rom 11:26), for "There shall come *out of Zion* the Deliverer; He shall turn away ungodliness from Jacob (Rom 11:26).[53]

As to their location, whether they are upon the earthly or the heavenly Mount Zion (Heb 12:22), Revelation 14:2-3 sheds some light. It says,

> And the sound which I heard was as harpers harping with their harps. And they [the harpers][54] are singing a new song in the presence of the throne and in the presence of the four living creatures and the elders: and no one is able to learn the song except the hundred forty-four thousand, the ones who have been purchased from the earth.[55]

The throne, the four living creatures, and the twenty-four elders picture a heavenly scene with its heavenly occupants and adornments. It has done so from chapters 4-5 onward, and it is difficult now to see this aggregation upon the earth. This strongly favors a location upon the heavenly Mount Zion (Heb 12:22) rather than a location upon the earthly one at the start of or during the millennial reign. J. B. Smith asserts:

> The Mount Zion ... cannot be the earthly Mount Zion as Bengel, Hengstenberg, and others have correctly shown because those who are standing there, hear and learn the song sounding from heaven,

[52]Smith, p. 208.

[53]Author's emphasis. Cf. Isaiah 59:20; Psalm 14:7.

[54]"The subject to *adousin* is of course not the 144,000 but the heavenly harpers" (Henry Alford, *The Greek Testament*, 4:684).

[55]Author's translation.

which is sung before the throne and the four living creatures and the elders (14:3). The Mount Zion in this instance, as in Hebrews 12:22, belongs to the heavenly Jerusalem.[56]

Be it on the heavenly or earthly sacred hill it is certain that these saints are no longer seen in the throes of the Tribulation. On this Alford's remark on Revelation 14:4 applies. He writes,

> *These are they who were not* [defiled with women]. The aor. shews that their course is ended and looked back on as a thing past: and serves to confute all interpretations which regard them as representing saints while in the midst of their earthly conflict and trial.[57]

With the above discussion still in mind, a look at the emphasis of this inset can lead to a conclusion with reference to the chronological aspect of this sight. The 144,000 were seen to have been sealed earlier in Revelation 7:1-8, and from chapters 8 through 13, furious judgments have been occurring against the ungodly while a terrible persecution of Israel and the saints takes place (11:7-10; 12:6, 13-17; 13:4-18). During the next four chapters, 15-18, more judgments will come forth. Amid this holocaust, lest the reader of little faith wonder concerning the latter end of the sealed ones, the Spirit who guides the writing of all Scripture, calms all doubts by showing the final portion of those who were earlier sealed—and all see that their portion is with Christ forever (Rev 14:4). It would seem that the point that the Spirit is attempting to make in this inset is not so much to show the readers the 144,000's exact geographical location, as it is to make manifest *their final destiny*.

If this be true, and it assuredly is, then chronologically speaking it must be concluded that this inset gives a picture, telescopically looking out into time, of the 144,000 safe with Christ after the fury of the Great Tribulation has run its course. Since they "follow the Lamb withersoever he goeth" (Rev 14:4)[58] they may be seen near Him, we may be certain, at the end of the Tribulation, during the

[56]Smith, p. 208.

[57]Alford, 4:248-49.

[58]About the words, "These are the ones who follow the Lamb withersoever he goeth" (Rev 14:4), Alford, 4:686, says: "The description has very commonly been taken as applying to the entire obedience of the elect, following the Lord to prison and to death, ... but this exposition is surely out of place here, where not their life of conflict, but their state of glory is described. The words, as Aug. (. . .), Andreas, Zullig, Stern, Dusterd, are used of special privilege of nearness to the Person of the Lamb in glory."

thousand years, and in the eternal state irrespective of whether this particular glimpse of them is caught on the heavenly or earthly sacred mount of Jerusalem.

THE HARVEST (REV 14:14-20)

Between the insets

After the episode concerning the 144,000 on Mount Zion (Rev 14:1-5), there come three angelic announcements that proclaim the everlasting gospel, the fall of Babylon,[59] and the doom of all who worship the Beast and receive his mark (Rev 14:6-12). Then a voice from heaven says,

> Write: Blessed are the dead who are dying in the Lord from henceforth. Yea, says the Spirit, in order that they might rest from their labors: for their works are following after them (Rev 14:13).[60]

Since this is said, not in one of the two episodes of Revelation 14, but between the two (between the inset concerning the 144,000 on Zion, vv. 1-5, and the harvest inset, vv. 14-20), chronologically its place seems clear. It is said after the sounding of the seventh trumpet (Rev 11:15-19), but before the spilling of the bowls which occurs well into the second 3½ years (chaps. 15-16). Thus the significance of this proclamation is that those who are about to die for Christ amid the carnage of the Beast's persecution in the second half of the week are of a certainty blessed and will find rest with Christ.

The harvest (Rev 14:14-20)

This inset, clearly taking up the picture of Joel 3:11-14, shows Christ, "one like a son of man," sitting on a white cloud with a golden crown upon his head and with a sharp sickle in his hand (v. 14). The sovereign Lord is thus ready to commence a severe judgment of reaping "for the harvest of the earth is ripe" [aorist passive of xērainō; literally, "dried up"[61]]. The time of this judgment, which will be performed by Christ (John 5:2-22) with angelic assistance (Rev 14:17-19; cf. Matt 13:39-43), can be discerned from verses 19-20 which read,

---

[59]The fall of Babylon will be discussed later in this chapter.
[60]Author's translation.
[61]Arndt, p. 550.

And the angel cast his sickle unto the earth, and gathered the vine of the earth and cast it into the great winepress of the wrath of God. And the winepress was trodden outside of the city, and blood came out of the winepress unto the bridles of the horses, for a distance of a thousand six hundred stadia.[62]

From the above verses, which tell the same story as Joel 3:9-16, the conclusion is unavoidable that,

> The allusion is plainly to the assembled nations in the valley of Jehoshaphat at which time the Lord will be revealed from heaven to smite the nations with the rod of His mouth, elsewhere designated as the Battle of Armageddon the actual fulfillment of which is recorded in Revelation 19:15. Cf. Isaiah 63:3; Jeremiah 25:30, 31; Joel 3:13b-16a.... The city is undoubtedly Jerusalem, for so the prophets declare, e.g., Joel 3:16; Zechariah 14:2, 3.[63]

The imagery observes the wicked armies of the whole earth who follow the Antichrist into the Valley of Jehoshaphat to engage in the final battle against Jerusalem, Israel, the saints, and God (Joel 3:9-16; Zech 14:1-4; Rev 16:12-14). They are beheld as so many grapes gathered into the wine vat for crushing. The treading of the winepress extends for a distance of 1,600 stadia (Rev 14:20), or about 184 miles.[64]

This same treading of the winepress is described in Isaiah 63:1-6 where God [Christ] is pictured as having his garments dyed red from the spattering of the blood of the wicked whom He is crushing. In Isaiah 63:1, the one treading the winepress is seen to come *from* Bozrah, Edom's capital. If this is taken as the southernmost point of the judgment at hand, and if it extends in a straight line through the region of the Valley of Megiddo and Mount Megiddo ("Armageddon" means "Mount Megiddo" in the Hebrew) for 184 miles, the 1,600 stadia of Revelation 14:20, then the line would reach to Tyre. Thus the winepress of God, wherein

[62]Author's translation.

[63]Smith, p. 221.

[64]Arndt, p. 771, is correct in stating that a stadium (*stadion*, Rev 14:20; an Attic one) equals 607 English feet, but incorrect in equating this figure to 192 meters (the length of an Olympic stadium, which equals 630.8 feet). The Attic stadium equals 607 feet, the equivalent to 185 meters. 1,600 of these Attic stadia equal 184 miles (607 ft/stadium × 1,600 stadia ÷ 5,280 ft/mi equals 184 mi). Recent printings of the Arndt & Gingrich lexicon have this error corrected.

A "furlong," as the KJV and ASV translate "stadium," is 220 yards, or 660 feet long. See "stadium" and "furlong" in *Webster's New Collegiate Dictionary*, rev. ed. (Springfield, Mass.: G. & C. Merriam Co., 1977).

the "grapes of wrath" are stamped out, seems to extend completely through Palestine from Bozrah in the Southeast to Tyre in the Northwest. Here Christ will destroy the armies of the Antichrist at His appearing at the close of the Tribulation (Matt 24:29-31; Rev 19:11).

THE DESTRUCTION OF BABYLON (REV 17-18)

The nature of "Babylon the Great"

Revelation 17 and 18 together describe the final destruction of "Babylon the Great" (17:5; 18:2). Before a chronological determination of the destruction of this entity can be made, it is necessary to first apprehend her nature.

In Revelation 17 she is pictured as "the great harlot that sitteth upon many waters" (v. 1). In the figure of a woman, which so often represents religion in the Scriptures (in Hosea, Gomer represents unfaithful Israel; Rev 12, the woman is Israel; Rev 19:7, the Bride is the true church; and in Rev 2:20 Jezebel seems to represent the papal church), here Babylon the Great is seen to be religion that has left the true God and committed fornication with the kings and people of the earth and whose fruit has been the persecution of the true saints (17:1-6). In Revelation 18 Babylon the Great is seen as a city, a great political capital, and as a world center of trade and business (18:10-11).

To this let it be added that her name "Babylon" shows that her origins reach back to the ancient foundations of organized iniquity (cf. Gen 10:8-10; 11:9); the titles "the great" and "queen" (Rev 17:5; 18:2, 7) show that she has been up to this time triumphant and mighty; and her label, "the great harlot" (17:1) designates her as not only being evil herself, but also as one who perverts multitudes of others unto wickedness.

Her endtime appearance in Revelation 17 as the final manifestation of the great harlot, is that of a worldwide false religious system—for she sits above "peoples, and multitudes, and nations, and tongues" (Rev 17:1, 15).[65] This future system no doubt shall include apostate Protestantism in an unholy amalgamation with the Roman Catholic organization, with the various other pagan religions also included. Such events as the 1955 and 1965 "Festi-

---

[65]Hoyt, "Apocalypse," p. 171.

vals of Faith," both held in the San Francisco Cow Palace, were ominous portents of this final form of the "Great Harlot." Besides being the final false religious system, Babylon is also the head-quarter city and motherland of this system (Rev 17:18).

Babylon the Great, be it rebuilt Babylon or Rome, shall appear in the Tribulation also as described in Revelation 18, as the great political and commercial capital of the world. As such it will be the capital of the kingdom of the Antichrist from the time that he becomes world ruler, which occurs at the middle of the week, until it is destroyed by God (Rev 16:10, 19; 18:2-24).

Thus, the Apocalypse in these Tribulation period chapters, 6-19, shows the following: Babylon is intimately connected with the satanically controlled Beast with seven heads and ten horns (17:3, 8-17 cf. 12:3). The Beast as a person is the Antichrist; and as a kingdom the Beast at the endtime represents the Revived Roman Empire.[66] The ten horns represent ten endtime kings (Rev 17:12).[67] On these ten horns of Revelation 17:12-17, Gaebelein observes, "They correspond to the ten toes on Nebuchadnezzar's image and [to the ten horns on] the fourth beast which Daniel saw coming out of the sea" (Dan 2:40-44; 7:19-28).[68]

All of the above is well summarized in Shattuck's explanatory paraphrase of Revelation 17:5 in which he seeks to exhibit the identity of "Babylon the Great."[69] He renders the verse as follows:

> And upon her [the great harlot's] forehead was written a symbolic name: *Babylon the great* ecclesiastical, political and commercial, diabolic world system which began in the ancient city of Babel, whose final manifestations will be in an Apostate World Church and in the world empire of the Antichrist, both of which will possess in their respective times the rebuilt city of Babylon, the mother of all false religions and cults the world will ever know and the source of every ensnaring object used by Satan to seduce men upon the earth.[70]

It need not cause any to wonder that the same city should be both a religious and political capital. Rome, Salt Lake City, and

---

[66]See chapter 1.

[67]See chapter 1.

[68]Arno C. Gaebelein, *The Revelation*, p. 103.

[69]Grant Duane Shattuck, "A Critical Investigation of Revelation 17:5," B.D. critical monograph.

[70]Ibid., p. 68. Author's emphasis. This paraphrase is the succinct conclusion of Shattuck's entire monograph.

Boston are modern examples of such a condition, and the ancient examples are legion.

With this understanding of the final Babylon, the two main chronological questions involved in Revelation 17 and 18 may now be asked. They are: (1) when does the destruction of the great harlot, the final system of false religion, occur (Rev 17)? and (2) when does the destruction of the political and commercial capital of Antichrist's kingdom, the city Babylon the Great, occur (Rev 18)? While answering these questions, other pertinent chronological data will be noted.

When Is the harlot of Revelation 17 destroyed?

The intent of Revelation 17 is given in the bowl angel's words to John at the outset of this episode. The angel said, "Come, I shall show to you the judgment (krima—"condemnation and punishment"[71]) of the great harlot that sits upon many waters." It is a proclamation of the coming final destruction of "false religion" which has ridden upon the great pagan empires of the ages.[72] Of course, this destruction can only take place at the time of the final manifestation of the great harlot which here is seen according to the futuristic outlook to occur during the Tribulation period.

Before the time of the harlot's fall can be set, four things must be first understood. These are:

First, it is clear that the ten horns which appear on the scarlet colored Beast of the Apocalypse (Rev 17:12-13), on Daniel's fourth beast (Dan 7:19-27), and as the ten toes of Daniel's image (Dan 2:40-44) are the ten kings of the Revived Roman Empire in the endtime.[73] Revelation 17:12, plainly says, "And the ten horns ... are ten kings. These rise to power before the Antichrist (Dan 7:20, 24), but when the Antichrist does rise, he soon in some way humbles three of these kings and then all ten are seen to give their unswerving allegiance to the Beast (Dan 7:19-27; Rev 17:12-13),[74] At this point in the chronology the words of Revelation 17:13 apply, "These [ten kings] are having one mind, and their power and authority they are giving to the Beast." This must occur at

[71]Arndt, p. 451.
[72]See the lengthy footnote (pp. 142-43) on the seven heads of the Beast, Revelation 13's inset vision.
[73]Binkley, pp. 48-54.
[74]Daniel 7:19-27 is quoted in chapter 1, Table 2.

least by the middle of the week when the Antichrist becomes the global despot (Rev 13:8).

Second, the germane chronological significance of Revelation 17:3 must be comprehended. This verse says, "and I saw a woman sitting upon a scarlet-colored beast, full of names of blasphemy, having seven heads and ten horns." Thus at the start of this scene the false religious system is seen already sitting astride the Revived Roman Empire, the satanic Beast who is now led by its seventh head. Though it may be questionable whether the rider is leading its mount, or if the mount is leading the rider, it is clear that the mount provides the means of locomotion for the one astride. That is, the Revived Roman Empire and the Antichrist carry the harlot church system with them.

Third, it is to be noted that the destruction of the harlot church comes at the hands of the ten kings and the Antichrist. Revelation 17:16-17 explains how this occurs. These verses declare,

> And the ten horns which thou sawest, and the beast, these shall hate the harlot, and shall make her desolate and naked, and shall eat her flesh, and shall burn her utterly with fire. For God did put in their minds to do his mind, and to come to one mind, and to give their kingdom unto the beast, until the words of God should be accomplished.

This description shows that the ten kings in alliance with the Antichrist shall in successive steps (hate, make desolate, eat, burn) totally destroy the false religious system. The reason for the ten kings doing this seems in verse 18 to be linked with their decision to give their kingdom, that is, their allegiance and power, to the Beast, the Antichrist. The *beast* in verse 18 must be the Antichrist as an individual and not the kingdom he heads, for how could ten kings already in the Revived Roman Empire give their kingdom over to the Empire? Clearly, they give their power to the Antichrist; and this delivery of power is connected with their helping him to burn the harlot church (vv. 16-17).

Fourth, it is to be remembered that after his resuscitation and his committing of the abomination of desolation in the middle of the week, the Antichrist declares himself to be this world's only god and becomes the supreme world dictator, persecuting all who refuse to obey and worship him (Rev 13:3-8ff).

Thus it has been seen that: (1) the Revived Roman Empire has ten kings, who, by the middle of the week, have yielded their power to the world ruler, the Antichrist;[75] (2) for a period, the harlot church and the Beast are yoked together; (3) the ten kings join the Beast in destroying the harlot church, and this alliance is related to the ten kings giving their kingdom to the Beast; and (4) after the middle of the week all must worship Antichrist as the earthly deity.

With these things in mind, the picture becomes clear once it is accepted that: (1) for the first half of the week the harlot church and the Beast are joined together for mutual advancement; but (2) at the middle of the week, when the Antichrist declares himself to be god (2 Thess 2:3-4), the ten kings join him and they destroy the harlot church; and then (3) from that time on the Antichrist, with the support of the ten kings, represents not only the sole rule, but also the sole religion until his destruction at Christ's coming at the end of the seven years.[76]

It should be noted that the scriptural record lucidly shows that in the first stage both Beast and harlot exist simultaneously (the false church and the Antichrist; Rev 17:3); in the second stage the Beast slays the harlot (Rev 17:16); and in the third stage the Beast rules alone until Christ comes (Rev 13:7-8; 19:19-20). The only item to be questioned is: *At what point* during the seven years does the Antichrist and his ten kings proceed to destroy the harlot? One point of time alone stands out when the Antichrist would come into conflict with the organized religious amalgamation, at the midpoint of the week when he declares himself to be god. Probably he does this at least partially in order to get rid of the great harlot whom he no doubt loathes as a rival for the supreme allegiance of the hearts of men.

The above advocated chronological system is in perfect harmony with all of the facts. It explains why the killing of the harlot by the ten kings is related to their giving their kingdom to the Beast (Rev 17:16-17). To cast in their lot with him they must worship *him* (cf. Matt 4:8-9), and therefore they can no longer worship with the great harlot's false system. This in turn is true because the great harlot's system must be an amalgamation of all

[75]It is no doubt by now plain to the reader that the middle of the week signifies more than merely the midinstant of the seven years. Since several key non-instantaneous events occur at this time it is not amiss to suggest that the "middle" and the "midpoint" of the week may comprehend a period of several days or more in length.

[76]Hoyt, "Apocalypse," p. 172.

world religions, probably a humanistic-pantheism, because her system is followed by "peoples, and multitudes, and nations, and tongues" (Rev 17:15). The harlot's system and that of the Beast are mutually exclusive—she permits all false worship; he tolerates no worship but that of himself (Rev 13:15; 2 Thess 2:3-4). The kings choose the Beast and burn the harlot.

Since Israel is worshiping safely in her rebuilt Temple during the first 3½ years (Dan 9:27; Matt 24:15ff; 2 Thess 2:3-4), the great harlot system must at least tolerate this worship of Jehovah and permit it to continue; but from the midpoint onward, the Beast will no longer tolerate it (Matt 24:15-22). Therefore, the midpoint of the week is the apt point at which the religious order of the Tribulation can make the transition from the harlot's toleration to the Beast's intolerance.

Thus it can be concluded that the judgment of the great harlot comes at the hands of Antichrist at the middle of the week or directly thereafter.[77]

Since the harlot is also a city (Rev 17:18), Babylon the Great (17:5), which is the headquarters and motherland of the false religious system, the fierce providential judgment of burning and desolation recounted in Revelation 17:16 at the hands of the Beast and the ten kings will no doubt ravage all in Babylon that pertains to the harlot. Thus at the middle of the week Satan has cast off the Harlot so that he, in the form of Antichrist, is worshiped directly—his iniquitous desire from the beginning (Isa 14:13-14; Matt 4:8-9; Rev 13:4).

When is the political and commercial Babylon of Revelation 18 destroyed?

The harlot having been destroyed at the middle of the week or directly thereafter, for the last 3½ years the city called "Babylon" is seen as the capital city of the kingdom of the Beast (Rev 16:10, 19; 17:18; 18:2-4, 9-10, 18-24). Whether this city is Rome, actual ancient Babylon rebuilt, or some other commercial metropolitan region is still debated, and may even be undiscoverable until the Tribulation period begins. Also, whether the image of the Beast

[77]Ibid.

(Rev 13:15) is located in Babylon, Jerusalem, Rome or some other place, Scripture does not reveal. In any case, this "Babylon" eventually does become the unrivaled commercial capital of the world (Rev 18:9-19). This is fitting. Since the god of this world is one of materialism, can its unholy capital in the Tribulation be any different?

As for Babylon's destruction, Revelation 18 is clear that it will occur extremely rapidly, that it will be by fire, and that it will be complete. This is seen in the following expressions taken from verses 2, 8-10, and 17-23:

> Fallen, fallen is Babylon the great, and is become a habitation of demons, and a hold of every unclean spirit, and a hold of every unclean and hateful bird.... in one day shall her plagues come, death, and mourning, and famine; and she shall be utterly burned with fire; ... the smoke of her burning ... for in one hour is thy judgment come ... for in one hour so great riches is made desolate ... and cried out as they looked upon the smoke of her burning ... for in one hour she is made desolate.... Thus with a mighty fall shall Babylon, the great city, be cast down, and shall be found no more at all ... and no craftsman, of whatsoever craft, shall be found any more at all in thee; ... and the light of a lamp shall shine no more at all in thee; and the voice of the bridegroom and of the bride shall be heard no more at all in thee.

As for the time of this great and swift inferno, the Scriptures are clear, as a comparison of Revelation 18:5 and 16:17-19's usages of the verb "to remember" shows:

> For her [Babylon's] sins have reached unto the heavens, *and God remembered* her unrighteous deeds (Rev 18:5).[78] And the seventh angel poured out his bowl ... and there occurred a great earthquake, so great a one occurred not since men were upon the earth, so mighty an earthquake [and] so great. And the great city went into three parts, and the cities of the nations fell. And Babylon the great *was remembered before God* to give to her the cup of the wine of the anger of His wrath (Rev 16:17-19).[79]

In Revelation 18:5 above, it is certain that God's remembering Babylon's unrighteous deeds signifies that "God remembered" them with judgment and destruction. It is not that they were ever forgotten, but that here at Babylon's just visitation all of these

[78]Author's translation.
[79]Author's translation.

deeds are called to witness that her destruction is just and deserving. In like manner, when Revelation 16:17-19, above, describes part of the effects of the seventh bowl of God's wrath, the significance of Babylon being then "remembered before God" is that she is judged with destruction at this time, at the pouring of the seventh bowl.[80]

From this, the final destruction of the great political and commercial capital city, Babylon, must occur at the time of the pouring out of the seventh bowl, which occurs very close to the end of the Tribulation.[81] That this is not synonymous with the time of the final end of the Antichrist at Christ's coming is certain for (1) he, Antichrist, is not in Babylon but in Palestine at the Lord's appearance (Zech 14:1ff; Rev 19:11-21); (2) it would be indeed surprising if the end of so mighty a figure were not even mentioned in Revelation 18 if he perished with Babylon; and (3) the fact that wicked men are left to lament the fall of Babylon (Rev 18:9-11) shows that the final end is not coincident with this city's destruction.[82]

Thus by the time of the end of the Tribulation, when the seventh bowl has been poured out, it may truly be said that, "It is done" (Rev 16:17). The kingdom and capital of the Beast are destroyed and the great harlot has been destroyed; all that remains to the earthly conflict is for Christ at His revelation (Rev 19:19-21) to vanquish the wicked assemblage of the Beast and his armies gathered at the end of the seven years at Armageddon. Then Satan himself will also be imprisoned and later destroyed (Rev 20:1-10).

THE MARRIAGE OF THE LAMB (REV 19:1-10)

> Husbands, love your wives, even as Christ also loved the church, and gave himself up for it; that he might sanctify it, having cleansed it by the washing of water with the word, *that he might present the church to himself a glorious church*, not having spot or wrinkle or any such thing; but that it should be holy and without blemish (Eph 5:25-27).[83]

> For I am jealous over you with a godly jealousy: *For I espoused you*

---

[80]This is true despite the fact that Revelation 18:5 uses the verb mnēmoneuō, "to remember," but Revelation 16:19 uses the similar verb mimnēskomai, "to recall to mind, to remember" (Arndt, pp. 524, 526-27). The two are quite similar and here have not only like sounds, but also essentially the same effect and meaning.

[81]See chapter 4, part C.

[82]Hoyt, "Apocalpyse," p. 178.

[83]Author's emphasis.

to one husband, that I might present you as a pure virgin to Christ (2 Cor 11:2).[84]

The time for the marriage of the Lamb has arrived, the time when the church is presented to Christ as a body officially and forever. Here the question shall be, When does the marriage occur, and when does the "marriage supper" mentioned in Revelation 19:9 occur?

Let it be noted that in the passage at hand, four successive "alleluias" are given forth with various announcements and proclamations surrounding each of them. These "alleluias" show that the passage is a united one, and that the entire scene is one of triumph, joy, and praise.

After the first "alleluia," it is said that God "hath judged the great harlot ... and he hath avenged the blood of His servants at her hand" (Rev 19:2). Then after a few verses the fourth "alleluia" is given and it is said,

> For the Lord our God, the Almighty, reigneth. Let us rejoice ... for the marriage of the Lamb is come, and his wife hath made herself ready. And it was given unto her that she should array herself in fine linen, bright and pure: for the fine linen is the righteous acts of the saints.... Blessed are they that are bidden to the marriage supper of the Lamb (Rev 19:6-9).

From all this it is observed that the marriage of the Lamb takes place at least *after* the great harlot has been overthrown. This conclusion is warranted by more than one factor.

First, *before the proclamation of the marriage* (Rev 19:7) it is plainly declared in Revelation 19:2 that God "hath judged the great harlot." Here the aorist of the verb krinō, "to judge," points to this event having been completed in the past. Likewise in the same verse it is said that the blood of God's servants has been avenged (exedikēsen). Here the aorist again points to a past action.

Second, the announcement, "for the marriage of the Lamb is come" (Rev 19:7 KJV), made after the great harlot is said to have been judged, shows that the time of the marriage has now at last arrived. Thus Revelation 19:1-9 indicates that the harlot is destroyed before the wedding is performed.

It is to be observed that it is in harmony with the declared joy and triumph of the occasion (Rev 19:1-7) that the Bride's rival, the

---

[84]Author's emphasis.

great harlot, who has shed so much of the saints' blood (17:6, 19:2), be judged and her false claims exposed before the marriage takes place.

It must also be concluded that the marriage takes place or at least begins *before* Christ comes with His saints at the end of the Tribulation (Rev 19:11-21). The evidence indicates that this is true because:

1. When the wedding is announced in Revelation 19:1-9 with its precursory proclamations, no mention is made of the Beast's downfall, but the overthrow of the harlot is proclaimed. Though the telling of the harlot's doom is fitting to the occasion, it must be remembered that a declaration of the Beast's fall would also be apropos because he wars against the Groom, Christ, and because he is a *greater* monster than the harlot (for he conquers the harlot, Rev 17:16; he lasts until the end of the period, Rev 19:20; and he is a personification of Satan himself, Rev 12:3 cf. 13:1). Why is the ruination of the harlot alone named? Answer: Because the Beast has not as yet been destroyed.

2. At the coming of Christ, His armies are wearing "shining-white clean linen" (Rev 19:14).[85] This is earlier described in Revelation 19:8 as the array of the Bride, the church, "radiant clean linen,"[86] and the "linen" is there expressly called "the righteous acts of the saints." If the marriage representation be adhered to, then this sight of the Bride and Groom publicly together with the Bride in wedding apparel would imply that the wedding has taken place already or is at least in progress.[87] Here it is to be recalled that the "marriage" between Christ and the church is more than just a mere *figure*; it is a *representation* of the actual relationship between the two.[88]

Thus the marriage, or at least its beginning, has been localized between the fall of the harlot and the Armageddon-coming of the Lord in the last 3½ years of the Tribulation.

One might wonder if the smoke mentioned in Revelation 19:3 after the second "alleluia" of the marriage proclamation can be used to assign the time of the marriage to an even more precise period, occurring definitely after the burning of the political capi-

[85]Author's translation.
[86]Author's translation.
[87]Although the saints, as individuals, were already with Christ at their deaths and at the rapture, here they appear at His side as an official body.
[88]See Newell, pp. 301-302, on this.

tal, Babylon, near the end of the Tribulation week (cf. Rev 18:9, 18). This, however, cannot be dogmatically affirmed, because the smoke referred to after the second "alleluia" could just as well be that of the harlot church alone after the ten kings have burned her in the middle of the week (Rev 17:16), and thus not necessarily include the smoke of the political capital which is itself later burned near the end of the week. In any case, what seems probable is that the marriage takes place in the last half of the seven year period.

If the rapture be pretribulational, as has been contended, then at a minimum this scheme allows the first 3½ years for the church to appear in heaven before the judgment seat of Christ (1 Cor 3:13-15; 2 Cor 5:10). This judgment is over by the time of the wedding, for Revelation 19:7 says, "and his wife hath made herself ready" (hētoimasen—aorist, showing past action).[89]

Further, concerning the marriage and the supper, it is known that,

> There are two parts to a Jewish wedding; one part in the Father's house (Luke 12:36), and the other part in the Bridegroom's house (Matt 25:1).[90]

In harmony with this, the wedding between Christ and the church is seen to begin in heaven. Then Christ with the church returns to earth, and upon earth the Lord shall serve a supper to the "friends of the bridegroom" (Rev 19:9 tells of the supper; Luke 12:35-37 says that the Lord shall serve it when He returns from the marriage; and John 3:29 tells of the existence of friends of the bridegroom). These friends, surely include among them the saved who are alive at the time of His return in glory (Matt 25:1-13; John 3:29; cf. Psalm 45). Pentecost suggests that the marriage supper may refer to the entire Millennium.[91]

Truly, as the Scripture records, "Blessed are they that are bidden to the marriage supper of the Lamb" (Rev 19:9). Oh, the wonders of grace that lie at the end of the road for God's people!

[89]Hoyt, "Apocalypse," p. 180.
[90]Ibid.
[91]J. Dwight Pentecost, *Things to Come: A Study in Biblical Eschatology*, p. 228. See his discussion on this topic, pp. 226-28.

This account tells of Christ sitting upon a white horse coming with His armies as "King of kings, and Lord of lords" to destroy the Beast and his armies, to rescue Israel and the saints, and to forcefully set up the long-awaited millennial reign.

Matthew 24:29-31 makes the time of this coming absolutely certain, saying,

> And *immediately after the tribulation of those days* the sun shall be darkened, and the moon shall not give her light, and the stars shall fall from the heaven, and the powers of the heavens shall be shaken. And then the sign of the Son of Man appear in heaven, and then all the tribes of the earth shall mourn [Zech 12] and they shall see the Son of Man coming upon the clouds of heaven with power and great glory: and He shall send His angels with a great sound of a trumpet and they shall gather His elect out of the four winds from the ends of the heavens unto their ends.[92]

Thus, this rescuing occurs "immediately after" the end of the seven year Tribulation. At this time, "the war of the great day of God, the Almighty" (Rev 16:14) takes place, with Christ annihilating the armies of the Beast that were lured to Armageddon starting at the time that the sixth bowl was spilled (Rev 16:13-16). Here the ancient prophecies of Isaiah 34 and 63:1-6; Joel 3; and Zechariah 12 and 14 are fulfilled when the Lord again fights for His children. Here the fowls of the air are summoned to eat the flesh of the mighty men of the wicked armies as well as the flesh of their royal leaders (Rev 19:17-21).[93] All of these mighty and earth shaking

[92]Author's translation.

[93]This invitation to the birds of the sky to sup at the end of the seven years as the banquet of the Lord (Rev 19:17-21) corresponds closely to the same invitation extended in Ezekiel 39:17-24. For this reason perhaps it is here fitting to say a word about that difficult section of Ezekiel 37-39. Concerning this highly debated portion, I make the following suggestions:

Ezekiel 37 first tells of God's future restoration of the nation of Israel; then chapters 38-39 supply some of the great details of how God will deliver her from those enemies which shall seek to destroy her in the latter days.

Ezekiel 38:1-17 describes the invasion of the land of Israel by Russia (Gog) and her satellites at a time when the nation of Israel is enjoying an outward peace (vv. 11, 14). This may be during the 3½ years of peace during the first half of the seven year peace covenant with Antichrist before he breaks it in the middle of the week (Dan 9:27), or it may be prior to this.

Ezekiel 38:18—39:7 speaks of God's intervention upon the scene and of His destruction of the northern invading hordes.

Ezekiel 39:8-16 tells of the seven months which will be required for the burying

events involved in Christ's triumphant appearance of Revelation 19:11-21 will surely come to pass "immediately after" the seven year judgment period runs its scheduled course (Matt 24:29-31).

Summary

By way of a visual summary of the contents of this chapter and the previous one, and in order to avoid needless repetition, Table 9 immediately following is offered so that the reader might be able to comprehend at a glance the general picture of the chronology of the Tribulation period.

of the destroyed forces from the North. When R. J. Dunzweiler and I visited Israel in Jan. 1968, just *seven months* after the June 6-11, 1967 war, we saw much wreckage still not yet cleared, and bodies still in *temporary* graves.

Ezekiel 39:17-29 corresponds with Revelation 19:17-21 and it describes the downfall of another last day satanic army seeking to wipe Israel from the map. Here the armies of the Antichrist are viewed as a great final sacrifice given to the fowls of the air. Since at the conclusion of this mass execution the house of Israel recognizes "from that day and forward" (Ezek 39:22) that Jehovah is her God, this must be dealing with Armageddon. This is so because at the conclusion of Armageddon's battle Israel turns en masse to the Saviour who for so many generations she has wickedly spurned (Zech 12:9-14). Also see Pentecost, pp. 340-58.

Table 9
The Chronology of the Tribulation

Ch	Before Trib or earlier	First half of the week	Middle of the week	Second half of the week	Immediately after the Tribulation
4	Throne scene in heaven				
5	Lamb worthy to open Book				
6		First 6 seals opened			
7		144,000 of Israel sealed		Great multitude out of the Great Trib: with Christ	
8		7th seal-------------? & first 4 trumps------------------------?			
9		5th & 6th--------------------------------? trumps			
10			7th trump: "Delay-----------------------------? no longer"		
11		The two witnesses prophesy 1260 days	2 witnesses slain & 7th trump	Gentiles tread down Jerusalem 42 months	

Table 9
The Chronology of the Tribulation

Ch	Before Trib or earlier	First half of the week	Middle of the week	Second half of the week	Immediately after the Tribulation
12	Dragon vs. Christ		Michael vs. Dragon	Dragon persecutes Israel 1260 days	
13		The Beast (Antichrist) rises	The Beast commits abomination & begins world-wide dominion	The Beast in power 42 months; all worship	
14				144,000 safe with the Lamb	Christ and sickle at Armageddon
15				Bowl angels appear	
16				Bowls of wrath	
17		Great Harlot (false religion) rides Beast	Great Harlot (false religion) destroyed		
18				Babylon burned	
19				The marriage of the Lamb	Christ's revelation & Armageddon

6
Revelation 20-22:
The Chronology of the Millennium and the Eternal State

THE MILLENNIUM (REV 20)

THE MILLENNIUM FOLLOWS THE SECOND COMING

The persuasion that the second advent takes place prior to the thousand year earthly reign of the Saviour, known as "premillennialism," has been assumed to be true at the outset of this study.[1] While this action has placed the necessity of defending this view against amillennial and postmillennial assailants beyond the scope of the examination at hand, it may not be out of place here to say a brief word on this immense topic.

The premillennial belief rejects the postmillennial idea that man by his own efforts will establish a kingdom of righteousness, which will last for a thousand years, at the conclusion of which Christ will come. Instead, it sees the world becoming progressively more lawless in preparation for the coming of the Antichrist, the Lawless One, who shall blaspheme God (2 Thess 2:3-4). It beholds Christ coming in fierce judgment to save the earth from unbridled violence, war, immorality, unbelief, and annihilation of all that is good (Rev 19:11-21). The premillennial view, unremittingly and unequivocally asserts that the postmillennialists err greatly when they construct their Kingdom without its King.

The premillennial belief likewise rejects the spiritualizing of the amillennialist who applies the Kingdom promises to the church and who sees in Isaiah's description of the wolf dwelling with the lamb (Isa 11:4-12) members of the church living in internal peace during this age. It rejects the amillennial (and postmillennial) concept that the first resurrection of Revelation 20 is spir-

[1]See Introduction.

itual while the second is literal. Premillennialism, supported by modern history, rejects the amillennial idea that Satan is *now* imprisoned when Revelation 20:3 says that the purpose of his imprisonment is that, "he should deceive the nations no more."

On Revelation 20:4-6 which tells of the first resurrection and the thousand year rule of the saints with Christ, Alford's bold words stand out as the classic refutation of all who, after looking at Revelation 20, seek to do away with the literal future millennial reign of Christ. He writes,

> It will have been long ago anticipated by the readers of this Commentary, that I cannot consent to distort words from their plain sense and chronological place in the prophecy, on account of any considerations of difficulty, or any risk of abuses which the doctrine of the millennium may bring with it. Those who lived next to the Apostles, and the whole Church for 300 years, understood them in the plain literal sense: and it is a strange sight in these days to see expositors who are among the first in reverence of antiquity, complacently casting aside the most cogent instance of consensus which primitive antiquity presents. As regards the text itself, no legitimate treatment of it will extort what is known as the spiritual interpretation now in fashion. If, in a passage where *two resurrections* are mentioned, where certain *psuchai ezēsan* ["souls lived"] at the first, and the rest of the *nekroi ezēsan* ["dead lived"] only at the end of a specified period after the first,—if in such a passage the first resurrection may be understood to mean *spiritual* rising with Christ, while the second means *literal* rising from the grave; —then there is an end of all significance in language, and Scripture is wiped out as a definite testimony to any thing. If the first resurrection is spiritual, then so is the second, which I suppose none will be hardy enough to maintain: but if the second is literal, then so is the first, which in common with the whole primitive Church and many of the best modern expositors, I do maintain, and receive as an article of faith and hope.[2]

Thus, it is the premillennial conviction, which now after two world wars, Korean conflict, Vietnam struggle, two Middle East wars, and an ever rising modern tide of evil looks to Christ's coming for His church (1 Thess 4:13-18) as the Blessed Hope, and Christ's coming with His church to set up His millennial Kingdom

---

[2]Henry Alford, *The Greek Testament*, 4:732-33. Alford's emphasis. On the four major theories concerning the first resurrection, literal, spiritual, ecclesiastical, and doctrinal, see E. B. Elliott, *Horae Apocalypticae*, 4:175-81.

(Rev 19:11—20:3) as the only promise of peace on earth this side of eternity.

THE CHRONOLOGY OF THE MILLENNIUM

Once the 1000 years, which are mentioned in each of the six verses throughout Revelation 20:2-7, are taken as literal, the chronological order of the six major events of Revelation chapter 20 is readily apparent. This order is as follows:

1. The Binding of Satan (vv. 1-3);
2. The First Resurrection (vv. 4-6);
3. The Thousand Year Reign (vv. 4-6);
4. The Loosening of Satan for a Little Season (vv. 7-8);
5. The Brief Rebellion (vv. 7-10);[3]
6. The Great White Throne, the Second Resurrection, and the Second Death (vv. 11-15).

That this is the correct order is manifestly seen from the clear time indications within the chapter itself. Verse 3 states that Satan is bound and imprisoned "in order that he might no longer deceive the nations, until the thousand years should be fulfilled: after these things it is necessary for him to be loosed for a short time."[4] From this it is undeniably plain that the thousand years occurs between the binding and subsequent loosing of Satan.[5]

That the first resurrection takes place before the thousand year period while the second resurrection follows this period, is shown by verses 4 through 6, especially by the words,

> And they lived and reigned with Christ a thousand years. The rest of the dead lived not until the thousand years were completed. This is the first resurrection.[6]

---

[3]See Jacob B. Smith, *A Revelation of Jesus Christ*, pp. 275-76, for an extremely worthwhile, though not exhaustive, discussion of this subject.

[4]Author's translation.

[5]See also Rev 20:7.

[6]Author's translation. The "first resurrection" (Rev 20:4-6) is a term that denotes the resurrection of all the redeemed. This has its focus at the start of the thousand years when: (1) at the rapture (1 Thess 4:13-18) those saints asleep in Christ are raised and the living believers are changed into their glorified bodies (1 Cor 15:51-52); and when (2) at the end of the Tribulation period, the Tribulation saints are raised (Rev 20:4), John F. Walvoord, *The Revelation of Jesus Christ*, pp. 285-300. Thus we have *one* "first resurrection" with at least two phases, and perhaps more.

It is likewise explicitly stated that the brief worldwide rebellion takes place after the thousand years have terminated and after Satan is loosed for his allotted short season. So verses 7 and 8 declare,

> And when the thousand years have been completed, Satan shall be loosed out of his prison, and he shall go out to deceive the nations in the four corners of the earth.[7]

Finally, it is evident that the postmillennial rebellion (vv. 7-9), which ends with the wicked being "devoured" (slain) by heavenly fire, must happen before the Great White Throne judgment and its attendant events take place. This rebellion simply could not be raised after the Great White Throne scene. This is because, by the end of the Great White Throne judgment, the wicked have been cast into the Lake of Fire, which is called the second death (vv. 11-15), and hence are no longer at liberty to conduct any kind of rebellion.

When all of the above clear locations are integrated within the account of Revelation 20, the order of the six major events just presented above must be regarded as the bonafide and genuine order.

THE ETERNAL STATE (REV 21-22)

The discussion here will seek to establish the answer to one primary question, Do the new heavens and earth and New Jerusalem come upon the scene before, during, or after the Millennium?

ARGUMENTS FAVORING THE NEW HEAVENS AND EARTH BEING PLACED
AFTER THE MILLENNIUM

> And I saw a new heaven and a new earth: for the first heaven and the first earth are passed away: and the sea is no more (Rev 21:1).

The arguments below point to the new heavens and earth appearing after the thousand years have been fulfilled. Objections to this view will be treated later in this same chapter.

First, the location of the vision of the new heaven and earth within the Apocalypse argues favorably for this view—although if

---

[7]Author's translation.

this argument were not followed by others, it would not in itself be conclusive.

The Apocalypse, following the pattern of Revelation 1:19, treats in chronological order (1) "the things which thou [John] sawest," the vision of the risen Christ in chapter 1; (2) "the things which are," the seven churches of this present age seen in chapters 2 and 3; and (3) "the things which shall come to pass hereafter," the Tribulation, the Millennium, and the eternal state. By Revelation 21:1 when the new heavens and earth come upon the scene, our present Christian age (chaps. 2-3), the Tribulation (chaps. 4-19), and the Millennium (chap. 20) have all appeared in an order corresponding to their correct chronological positions. In fact, from Revelation 19:11 to the end of chapter 20, the events described march forward in strict chronological succession; the second coming of Christ with His saints, the destruction of the armies of the Beast, the binding of Satan, the thousand year reign, the loosing of Satan, the final rebellion, the destruction of the rebellious ones, the doom of Satan, the second resurrection, the Great White Throne judgment, and the casting of the lost into the Lake of Fire. Then, in the next verse, Revelation 21:1, the new heavens and the new earth appear. In the verse following, 21:2, New Jerusalem is seen descending down upon the new earth. Needless to say, its descent must *follow* the creation of the new earth upon which it comes to rest.

Thus, since event after event appears in strict chronological succession, from Christ's coming as Judge (Rev 19:11ff), through the events of the Millennium and after (Rev 20), the appearance of the new heavens and earth presumably ought to be taken as the next event in chronological order *unless* there is scriptural indication to the contrary to prove that the series terminates its chronological rigidity between 20:15 and 21:1 without giving any indication to this effect. This argument appears to be even stronger when it is noted that the last nine verses of chapter 20 (vv. 7-15), describe postmillennial happenings. The sum of this argument is that the *prima facie* presentation of the sacred account gives the impression that the new earth comes into being after the Millennium. The question now is, Can this first impression be sustained under closer scrutiny?

Second, from theological and logical considerations it seems to me that the time of the new creation must be placed after the Millennium.

Revelation 21:3-5 provides the context of the coming of the new heavens and earth and of the New Jerusalem. The words of these verses are uttered only in light of the new relationships between God and redeemed man which although started at Calvary only come into final fulness with the advent of the new creation and the coming of the celestial city which descends upon the new earth. God is now seen dwelling in manifest presence with born-again man forever on earth. So Revelation 21:3-5 declares,

> And I heard a great voice out of the throne saying, Behold, the tabernacle of God is with men, and he shall dwell with them, and they shall be his peoples, and God himself shall be with them, and be their God: and he shall wipe away every tear from their eyes; and death shall be no more; neither shall there be mourning, nor crying, nor pain, any more: the first things are passed away. And he that sitteth on the throne said, Behold, I make all things new.

If these things occurred at any time prior to the rebellion at the end of the thousand year millennial period, could it be said that, "death shall be no more" (Rev 21:4)? The answer is obvious. The statement, "death shall be no more," can only come *after* the Great White Throne judgment, which itself follows the Millennium, for the judgment of the Great White Throne is specifically called, "The second death" (Rev 20:14). Clearly, these "new" things come into being after the Great White Throne which immediately follows the Millennium.

"Behold, I make all things new" (Rev 21:5) is said in a context which speaks of there no longer being any tears, death, mourning, crying, or pain with "the first things" having "passed away" (Rev 21:4). The absence of these former characteristics that mark the *results of sin* is the very thing which marks the newness of the creation. This is the element which unifies all of the new creation—the absence of any taint of sin or its effects.

Thus the text portrays the new, perfect and eternal order coming into existence *after* the sin problem has forever been put away. This occurs not at the start of or during the Millennium when the sin problem is *controlled* by Christ's rule with a rod of iron (Psalm 2:9), but after the Great White Throne judgment, following the Millennium, when sin and sinners are eternally put out of the liberated universe.[8] The point is that the new creation pictures "absolute perfection" which condition is clearly not a millennial one.[9]

Third, Scott argues in favor of placing the new creation after the thousand years by maintaining that the words of Revelation 21:1, "For the first heaven and the first earth have passed away," have "undoubted reference" to the statement in the previous chapter which there describes a postmillennial event (Rev 20:11, "From whose face the earth and the heaven fled, and a place was not found for them.")[10]

The verb used in 20:11, *pheugō*, "to flee," is used in Revelation 16:20, "And every island fled," when speaking of physical earthly masses being violently changed and moved, so it is quite within the Greek verb's bounds to refer to the heaven and earth fleeing, signifying a vast physical change such as the renovation of the old to the new order. Yet could Revelation 20:11 with its heaven and earth fleeing be a metonymy only signifying the fearful flight of the inhabitants of heaven and earth?

On this argument Buswell states his strong conviction thusly:

> This [Rev 20:11; 21:1] is language as clear and as strong as I can imagine language to be. If the statement, "This X, Y, and Z are gone, and their place cannot be found, but there are new X, Y, and Z," does not indicate numerical otherness, how can human language indicate it?[11]

Fourth, at the sight of the new creation, John the seer observes a startling absence, "And there is no longer the sea" (Rev 21:1).[12] This fact adds its weight to argue that the new order of heaven and earth follows the Millennium. In the words of Smith,

> The statement, *and there was no more sea*, shows that the reference is to the eternal age, for the *sea* is repeatedly mentioned as existing in passages pertaining to the kingdom age. Psalm 72:8; Isaiah 11:9; 60:5; Ezekiel 47:10, 20; 48:28; Zechariah 9:10; 14:8.[13]

[8]This alone renders absurd the Jehovah Witness assertions that the new heavens were created in A.D. 1914 and the new earth in A.D. 1919. *New Heavens and A New Earth* (Brooklyn: Watchtower Bible and Tract Society, Inc., 1953), pp. 322-23.

[9]J. Oliver Buswell, Jr., *A Systematic Theology of the Christian Religion*, 2:522-26. So even R. H. Charles, *A Critical and Exegetical Commentary on the Revelation of St. John*, 2:200.

[10]Walter Scott, *Exposition of the Revelation*, p. 405. Author's translation of verses.

[11]Buswell, 2:533.

[12]Author's translation.

[13]Smith, p. 281. See also Scott, p. 406.

Fifth, along with the above positive arguments, the negative argument must be noted with Hoyt, who observes that, "There seems to be no reason why these two chapters [20 and 21] should be regarded as describing something during the Millennium."[14] The point is that not only are there strong arguments favoring the locating of the new heavens and earth after the Millennium, but also there seems to be no commanding arguments to be found anywhere, once the futuristic approach has been established, to require the new heaven and earth to commence at the start of the thousand years. It would have been quite in order for chapter 21 to have returned to describe the millennial age (which the old Testament prophets have already well described for us, Isa 11:4-13), but it appears that the sacred account has chosen to leave the Millennium and the immediate events after it to chapter 20 and to go on in chapters 21-22 to exhibit to us the wonders of the eternal state. This claim calls for the next section which comes below.

NEW JERUSALEM FOLLOWS THE MILLENNIUM

> And I saw the holy city New Jerusalem descending out of heaven from God, having been prepared as a bride who has been adorned for her husband (Rev 21:2).[15]

Only One Descent. Before investigating the issue at hand directly, the arrangement of this account should be heeded. Revelation 21:1—22:5 tells of the new world with its new heavens, new earth, and new Jerusalem. Revelation 21:1-5 describes the first sight of these three new entities and tells of the perfect state which will surround them; Revelation 21:6-8 contains a hortatory interjection; and Revelation 21:9—22:5 again takes up the description of the city New Jerusalem, whose descent was earlier recounted in 21:2, only here the city is beheld from a different angle (21:10) and its characteristics and contents are recited in breathtaking detail.

> And he [the angel] carried me away in spirit upon a great and high mountain, and he showed to me the holy city Jerusalem descending out of heaven from God, having the glory of God (Rev 21:10-11) [16]

It must not be for a moment thought from the above Scripture that

---

[14]Herman A. Hoyt, "Apocalypse," p. 187.
[15]Author's translation.
[16]Author's translation.

a different descent from that described in 21:2 (quoted previously) is here indicated in 21:10-11. The words are so similar that it is here untenable to see the two otherwise undifferentiated descriptions, that of 21:2 and 21:10, as telling of the descents of different cities or even the same city at different times, one being premillennial and the other being postmillennial. The two statements read literally in their original word order as follows:

Revelation 21:2, *the city the holy Jerusalem new I-saw descending out-of the heaven from the God.*
Revelation 21:10, and he-showed to-me *the city the holy Jerusalem descending out-of the heaven from the God.*[17]

Clearly here is a literary and teaching device like the one used in the first two chapters of Genesis. There after the overall view of creation was given in Genesis 1, including a brief synopsis of the creation of man on the sixth day (Gen 1:26-29), in Genesis 2 the narrative returns to the creation of man and describes it in greater detail in connection with the Garden of Eden. Here in Revelation 21-22 the identical thing is done. After Revelation 21:1-5 recounts the bringing to pass of the new creation with a brief mention of the descent of the holy celestial city, then 21:9—22:5 returns to recount in detail the wonders of New Jerusalem. In both cases, in Genesis and in Revelation, after the overall view of the creation was given along with comments about it, the sacred pen returned to give a fuller account of the most beloved and important aspect of the creation—in Genesis the return was to *man*, in Revelation it was to the *New Jerusalem*.

The Descent Follows the Millennium. That the coming down of the New Jerusalem occurs after the thousand years is seen from the following particulars:

First, since the arguments given above show that the new heavens and earth come into being after the Millennium, the possibility that the New Jerusalem might descend from heaven any earlier seems out of the question. The sheer order of the presentation of events prevents such a possibility. First a new heaven and a new earth is seen, then a new capital city, New Jerusalem, is observed to descend (Rev 21:1-2). It is evident that the *new city*

[17]Eberhard Nestle, Erwin Nestle, and Kurt Aland, *Novum Testamentum Graece,* Revelation 21:2, 10. Author's translation.

descends only upon the *new* earth, and not upon the *old* earth. Manifestly everything here is new, "for the first things are passed away ... Behold, I make all things new" (Rev 21:4-5). Without further laboring, this point appears to be conclusive.

Second and third, the first two reasons given for the locating of the new heavens and earth after the thousand years also apply here, (1) the description of New Jerusalem's descent occurs *after* the Apocalypse has already treated the events of the Christian age, the Tribulation, the Millennium, and the rebellion immediately following the thousand years (Rev 1-20); and (2) the description of the new world, including the city of New Jerusalem, in 21:1-5, pictures a time of absolute perfection when sin and its effects no longer are present, which condition is not a millennial one, but one that pertains only to the eternal state following the Millennium. Thus the perfect and sinless city (21:27; 22:3-5) beheld in chapters 21-22 cannot be a millennial one.

Fourth, New Jerusalem has no Temple in it, for a free unhindered access to God is there present (Rev 21:22).[18] This could not be a millennial condition when sin is merely controlled rather than eradicated; it is the condition of the perfect eternal state. If the form of worship described in Ezekiel 40-48 is to be ever literally fulfilled, as many competent premillennial Bible teachers believe, this must occur in the Millennium,[19] for the absence of a Temple in this city indicates that the perfect state has arrived, and that consequently the city is not a millennial one, but one of the enduring eternal order.

OBJECTIONS

Before closing this subject it is necessary to inquire as to why some do not agree that the new heaven and new earth come into existence *after* the Millennium, and that the New Jerusalem, likewise, makes its descent *after* the Millennium.

One reason for many, perhaps even for most, who hold the view that Revelation 21-22 return again to the millennial picture is aptly stated by Buswell who writes,

> I have diligently sought to understand the reasoning which lies back of this opinion [that chs. 21-22 deal with the Millennium], and

[18]Scott, p. 423.
[19]Buswell, 2:537.

I am convinced that it is largely based upon the theory (held by Warfield and many others) that the book of Revelation is made up of recapitulation, or extended passages which repeat from different points of view what has been said before.[20]

Buswell here rightly speaks out against the idea that chapters 21-22 *must* contain a recapitulation of the millennial scene spoken of in chapter 20. While chapters 21-22 could have contained a return to the millennial scene, the above investigation of this possibility seems to me to weigh firmly against it.

A second reason is stated by Culver, who desires to show that the cataclysmic creation of the new heavens and earth takes place at the commencement of the thousand years. He builds upon the following assertion which he makes:

> If anyone should argue that some of the passages speak of disturbances at the beginning of the Millennium and others of disturbances at its close, he should read Hebrews 12:26 (quoting Haggai 2:6) in which the Lord distinctly promises, Yet once more [not twice] I will make to tremble not the earth only, but also the heavens.[21]

This unique claim is hardly tenable. The words, "yet once more" (*epī hapax*) here in effect signify, "yet once *finally* [in the future]," rather than "once but not twice."[22] Thus this saying cannot be used to preclude any prior lesser shakings of the heavens and earth before the final cataclysm of 2 Peter 3:10. In fact Christ Himself in Luke 21:11 clearly predicts "earthquakes" (plural) and "terrors and great signs from heaven" (plural) *before* His coming, and these certainly do not refer to the great catastrophic change which will later usher in the new heavens and earth (Luke 21:11, 25-27). The trembling of the earth spoken of in Hebrews 12:26 points to the final removal of the old order, and all agree with Culver that *this* unique cataclysm will not occur twice.

---

[20]Ibid., p. 526. Buswell mentions Zahn in connection with this opinion. Cf. Theodor Zahn, "The Writings of John." In *Introduction to the New Testament*, translated by M. W. Jacobus et al., 3:374-401.

[21]Ibid., 2:526-27, citing Robert D. Culver, *Daniel and the Latter Days*, (Englewood Cliffs, N. J.: Revell, 1954), pp. 177-89. The words in brackets represent the belief of Culver.

[22]Ibid.

Thus Culver's syllogism is as follows:[23]

1. There is to be only one future "trembling" of the heavens and earth (Heb 12:26).
2. The heavens and earth will experience a "trembling" at Christ's premillennial coming (Matt 24:29).
3. The heavens and earth will experience a "trembling" at their renovation (Heb 12:26; 2 Pet 3:10).
4. Therefore, the "trembling" at Christ's premillennial coming (Matt 24:29) and the "trembling" at the renovation of the heavens and earth (2 Pet 3:10) must be one and the same event.

This is a non sequitur because (1) premise two is false in its defining of the heavenly events which surround Christ's coming as a "trembling" of the heavens and earth of the same type as that when the former creation is done away with; and (2) as has been stated above, premise one errs, as Culver uses it, because the declaration of one future final "trembling" of the world does not preclude other "tremblings" of a different type or of a lesser magnitude prior to the final one.

In addition to the one above, it has already been seen in this study that the events in the heavens and earth which occur at Christ's coming at the end of the Tribulation are distinctly different both in time and type from the destruction of this present world by fire as described in 2 Peter 3:10.[24]

Another reason for some questioning the making of the descent of the New Jerusalem a postmillennial event lies in Isaiah 65:17-25 and perhaps also in 66:22-24. The problem is that here Isaiah plainly speaks of the creation of "new heavens and a new earth" (v. 17) and also in the same passage declares, "for the child shall die a hundred years old, and the sinner being a hundred years old shall be accursed" (v. 20). This latter saying must clearly refer to the Millennium, for Revelation 21:4 declares in connection with the new creation and the New Jerusalem that "death shall be no more."

It should at once be seen that if Isaiah is speaking about the new world, and he speaks of death within it, then there is a direct

[23]This syllogism is the writer's reduction of Culver's reasoning into steps. Of course, my disagreement with Culver on this point (as many will no doubt differ from me on points) in no way should suggest any attack on the individual or on the many other things that he believes. The same is true toward the many other sound expositors with whom I have been caused from time to time to disagree.

[24]See chapter 4, part D.

contradiction between Isaiah and Revelation 21:4, which teaches that death is nonexistent in the new world. What then is the solution? The solution is relatively simple. Isaiah is seen describing the new order in Isaiah 65:17 where God says,

> For, behold, I create new heavens and a new earth; and the former things shall not be remembered, nor come into mind.

In 65:20-25, Isaiah blends into his vision a glimpse also of the millennial conditions and in connection with them speaks of death.[25] On the device used here Smith writes,

> This introversion of prophetic passages, i.e., the mention of first fulfillment last and last fulfillment first, is no exception in the Old Testament Scriptures. A notable example occurs in the last two verses [of the Old Testament]. Malachi 4:5 speaks of "the great and dreadful day of the Lord"; while in verse 6, "... he shall turn the heart of the fathers to the children ..." As it happens, the last prophecy of the Old Testament is the first to be fulfilled in the New. In Luke 1:17 occurs Gabriel's message to Zacharias: "And he shall ... turn the hearts of the fathers to the children"; whereas "that great and notable day of the Lord" is mentioned first in Acts 2:20, which evidently still awaits fulfillment.[26]

In like manner can Isaiah 66:22-24 be divided.[27]

Clearly the case for making the New Jerusalem and the new order of Revelation 22:1—22:5 synchronous with the thousand years of Revelation 20:1-6 based upon Isaiah's mentioning of both in the same passage is inadequate. As it has been often observed, the Old Testament prophets often weave the mountain peaks which they spy out in their prophetic vision into one integrated tapestry without indicating the long valleys of time, invisible to their eyes, that stretch between the peaks (Luke 4:16-21 cf. Isa 61:1-2).

CONCLUSION CONCERNING THE NEW CREATION

In light of the reasons given above for placing the new heavens,

---

[25]Buswell, 2:518. Smith, p. 281, however, assigns Isaiah 65:17 alone to the postmillennial new order, and sees vv. 18-25 as millennial. In either case, the above solution is still true.

[26]Smith, p. 281.

[27]See Buswell, 2:511-22ff for an exhaustive analysis of Isaiah 61-66 with respect to the new heavens and earth.

new earth, and New Jerusalem as part of the new, perfect, sinless, eternal postmillennial order; and in view of the lack of cogency of the objections to this view, it is concluded that these wonderful entities recounted with awe in Revelation 21:1—22:5 are not part of the grand, yet imperfect millennial rule, but that they follow that wicked rebellion which ends the thousand years, and subsequently endure forever as part of the imperishable everlasting state.[28]

[28]Since the remainder of the Apocalypse, 22:6-21, is made up of the Epilogue which contains sundry admonitions and promises without chronological data per se, the body of this publication's discussion is ended here.

Conclusion

At this point, the problems concerning the chronological structure of the Apocalypse have been studied and solutions to those problems have been offered. All that remains to be done is to summarize the findings, comment on the degree of certainty with which the findings are put forth, and observe the significance of the findings.

Due to the nature of this particular study, with its discussion of the individual questions being strictly compartmentalized into chapters, it will not be necessary here to repeat the reasoning behind the conclusions. Anyone who desires a more detailed conclusion on any issue or the reasoning behind any finding, may consult the Contents.

As to the major findings of this study, in the Introduction it was pointed out that this examination was begun from the conservative viewpoint, holding to the grammatico-historico-theological method of hermeneutics, assuming that the premillennial position is correct, accepting Christ's coming as pretribulational, and observing that a distinction does in fact exist in God's program between the church of today and national Israel.

In the first chapter the various approaches to the Apocalypse were scrutinized. The result of this pursuit was the discovery that the critical, allegorical, and preterit views were seen to be wholly inadmissible, and the historical and topical schemes, although they had some merit, were nevertheless also untenable theories. Only the futuristic approach, which interprets Revelation chapters 6-19 as pertaining to that yet future seven year Tribulation period, Daniel's seventieth week, was seen adequately both (1) to allow the prophetic portions of Daniel, the Olivet Discourse, and the Apocalypse to harmonize; and (2) to meet the requirements of the chronological specifications of Revelation. This conclusion was arrived at with an overwhelming sense of certainty.

In the second chapter, because of the observed correspondences that existed between the course of this age and the seven churches of Revelation 2-3 and for other reasons, it was concluded that a latent prophecy of the course of the Christian age was placed by God in the messages to the seven churches. Thus these congregations were seen not only to be historical and representative, but also prophetic. It was also concluded that while churches of all seven of the types, persecuted like that of Smyrna and faithful like that of Philadelphia, have always existed and do exist now, nevertheless the tenor of the professing church today is basically Laodicean. These findings, when *carefully* enunciated, as was here done in the second chapter, were found not to conflict with the truth in the imminent return of the Saviour for His church.

In the third chapter which investigated Revelation 4-5, it was seen that the reception of the seven-sealed book by the Son takes place directly before the Tribulation period begins. The weight of the evidence also pointed to the already seated and crowned twenty-four elders as being identified as representing the raptured church in heaven. Other arguments were seen to corroborate this view.

In the fourth chapter inquiry was made as to the temporal relationship within and among the three series of judgments that dominate the seven year Tribulation period (Rev 6-19), the seals, trumpets, and bowls. It was unmistakably observed that *within* each of the series the judgments were unloosed successively, and that once the various judgments were released, they continued on in their effects both during and after other subsequent judgments were being sent forth.

Concerning the relationship *among* the judgments, it was concluded that the mass of the evidence demanded that they be understood as three *different successive* series, rather than either (1) three accounts of the same series, or (2) three different series released simultaneously. Their order was that of seals first, trumpets next, and bowls last. The seven trumpets were seen to come forth out of the seventh seal, and the seven bowls were seen to proceed out of the heavenly temple which in turn was a direct product of the seventh trump. The seals were assigned to the first 3½ years, the bowls to the last 3½ years, and the trumpets between the two.

In connection with this conclusion, certain serious problems and objections were considered at great length. Although every question may not have been forever settled in this study concerning these problems, yet the solutions discovered were regarded as providing highly satisfactory answers. In light of these problems, finding adequate solutions, and in the face of the evidence recounted in the fourth chapter for the three series following one upon another in succession, this conclusion is offered with a great degree of confidence.

The aim of the fifth chapter was to complete the picture of the chronology of the Tribulation period by discovering the time period that was pertinent to each of the inset visions of chapters 6-19. This was done with a great deal of certainty in every case. The precise chronological assignments of the sundry insets and the chronological picture of the Tribulation period as a whole may be seen on Table 9.

In the final chapter, the sixth, the chronology of the Millennium and of the eternal state, Revelation 20-22, was studied. It was concluded that the events of these times would unfold in this order: the binding of Satan; the first resurrection; the thousand year reign; the postmillennial loosing of Satan for a little season; the brief rebellion; the events of the Great White Throne, the second resurrection, and the second death; the creation of the new heavens and the new earth, and the descent of the New Jerusalem from heaven. This order, with its placing of the new creation and the coming down of the celestial city after, not during, the Millennium, seems to be the true representation of the teaching of the Apocalypse—and it is harmonious with the rest of Sacred Writ. It is therefore offered with much confidence.

The significance of these findings is manifold. They reveal the basic correctness of many of today's expositors of Revelation who present to their congregations His premillennial coming and the futuristic approach to Revelation with the seals, trumpets, and bowls occurring successively in that order, and with new creation and the New Jerusalem coming after the Millennium. Many who have proclaimed and who have written in this manner have never gone into great detail in justifying their chronology, and some come to correct conclusions on the basis of incorrect or inadequate reasons. These who have arrived at this basic chronology, especially those who have arrived at it despite inadequate investigation, show that men are not led far astray when they follow in general the *prima facie* presentation of the Apocalypse's chronology without entering the study with *a priori* recapitulation or other theories to justify.

The results of this study show that while events on earth may progressively worsen until Christ comes for His church and that "man of lawlessness be revealed" (2 Thess 2:3) commencing the fearful seven year Tribulation period, yet through it all God will save multitudes by His grace. Though the wickedness of man may abound, through Christ grace shall much more abound (Rom 5:20).

Thus in the face of coming calamities let it be remembered with confidence that our God is the One, "declaring the end from the beginning, and from ancient times things that are not yet done; saying, My counsel shall stand, and I will do all my pleasure" (Isa 46:10).

All shall end well! Righteousness shall triumph, evil shall be judged, and grace will reap its bounty. These clear teachings are the strength of the wonderful Apocalypse; and even those sincere believers who misinterpret its chronology reap much great blessing by learning these unmistakable truths and are therefore able to face the future with prayerful confidence knowing that our God, not fate nor man, is at the helm of the universe.

May the Lord who revealed the Apocalypse to John guide reader and writer alike in the understanding of that portion of the future which He has seen fit to reveal. May all praise Him who still with open arms at the end of the Apocalypse says, "And he that is athirst, let him come: he that will, let him take the water of life freely" (Rev 22:17).

May each reader end this study with the prayer of John, "Amen, come Lord Jesus" (Rev 22:20).

Selected Bibliography

Books

Alford, Henry. *The Greek Testament*. Chicago: Moody, 1958. Vol. 4, *Hebrews-Revelation*.

Arndt, William F., and Gingrich, F. Wilbur. [Walter Bauer] *A Greek-English Lexicon of the New Testament and Other Early Christian Literature*. Chicago: U. of Chicago, 1957.

Barnes, Albert. *Daniel*. 2 vols. Grand Rapids: Baker, 1959.

———. *Revelation*. Grand Rapids: Baker, 1949.

Brunson, Alfred. *A Key to the Apocalypse*. Cincinnati: Walden & Stowe, 1881.

Bullinger, E. W. *The Apocalypse: The Day of the Lord*. 3rd ed., London: Eyre & Spottiswoode, 1935.

Buswell, J. Oliver, Jr. *A Systematic Theology of the Christian Religion*. Vol. 2. Grand Rapids: Zondervan, 1962.

Charles, R. H. *A Critical and Exegetical Commentary on the Revelation of St. John*. The International Critical Commentary, vols. 1-2. New York: Scribner, 1920.

Elliott, E. B. *Horae Apocalypticae*. 2nd ed., rev. 4 vols. London: Seeley, 1846.

The Englishman's Greek Concordance of the New Testament. 9th ed. London: Samuel Bagster and Sons, 1903.

Farrar, F. W. *The Early Days of Christianity*. New York: Funk & Wagnalls, 1883.

Field, Grenville O. *Opened Seals-Open Gates: A New Exposition of the Book of Revelation*, n.d.

Froom, LeRoy Edwin. *The Prophetic Faith of Our Fathers: The Historical Development of Prophetic Interpretation*. 4 vols. Washington: Herald, 1946-54.

Gaebelein, Arno C. *The Revelation*. New York: Our Hope, 1915.

Harrison, Norman B. *The End: Re-Thinking the Revelation*. Minneapolis: Harrison, 1941.

Hendriksen, W. *More Than Conquerors: An Interpretation of the Book of Revelation*. Grand Rapids: Baker, 1960.

Hengstenberg, E. W. *The Revelation of St. John*. 2 vols. Translated by Patrick Fairbairn. New York: Corter, 1853.

Hodge, Charles. *Systematic Theology*. 3 vols. New York: Scribner, 1872.

Hoyt, Herman A. *The Glory: An Exposition of the Book of Revelation*. Winona Lake, Ind., 1953.

Humberd, R. I. *The Book of Revelation*. 6th ed. Flora, Ind.: R. I. Humberd, n.d.

Ironside, Harry A. *Lectures on the Book of Revelation*. New York: Loizeaux, 1919.

Jamieson, R.; Fausset, A. R.; and Brown, D. *Commentary Practical and Explanatory on the Whole Bible*. Grand Rapids: Zondervan, 1962.

Kelly, William. *Lectures on the Book of Revelation*. rev. ed. London: Morrish, 1871.

Kepler, Thomas S. *The Book of Revelation*. New York: Oxford U., 1957.

Kuiper, B. K. *The Church in History*. Grand Rapids: Eerdmans, 1951.

Kuyper, Abraham. *The Revelation of St. John*. Translated by John Hendrik de Vries. Grand Rapids: Eerdmans, 1935.

Larkin, Clarence. *The Book of Revelation*. Philadelphia: Clarence Larkin Estate, 1919.

Lenski, R.C.H. *The Interpretation of St. John's Revelation.* Columbus, O.: Wartburg, 1943.

Makrakis, Apostolos. *Interpretation of the Revelation of St. John the Divine.* Translated by A. G. Alexander. Chicago: Hellenic Christian Educational Society, 1948.

Mauro, Philip. *The Patmos Visions: A Study of the Apocalypse.* Boston: Hamilton, 1925.

McClain, Alva J. *The Greatness of the Kingdom.* Grand Rapids: Zondervan, 1959.

McDowell, Edward A. *The Meaning and Message of the Book of Revelation.* Nashville: Broadman, 1951.

Morris, M. A. *Prophecy and Revelation.* 2nd ed. Elgin, Ill.: Brethren, 1937.

Nestle, Eberhard; Nestle, Erwin; and Aland, Kurt. *Novum Testamentum Graece.* 23rd ed. Stuttgart: Privileg. Württ., 1957.

Newell, William R. *The Book of The Revelation.* Chicago: Moody, 1935.

Pentecost, J. Dwight. *Things to Come: A Study in Biblical Eschatology.* Findlay, O.: Dunham, 1958.

Ramsay, W. M. *The Letters to the Seven Churches of Asia.* New York: Armstrong, 1909.

Randall, T. et al. *Revelation.* The Pulpit Commentary, edited by H. D. M. Spence and Joseph S. Exell, vol. 51. rev. ed. New York: Funk & Wagnalls, n.d.

Robertson, Archibald Thomas. *A Grammar of the Greek New Testament in the Light of Historical Research.* 4th ed. New York: Harper and Brothers, 1923.

Schaff, Philip. *History of the Christian Church.* 8 vols. Grand Rapids: Eerdmans, 1910.

Scofield, C. I. *The Scofield Reference Bible.* New York: Oxford U., 1909.

Scott, Walter. *Exposition of the Revelation.* 2nd ed., rev. New York: Our Hope n.d.

Seiss, Joseph Augustus. *The Apocalypse.* 3 vols. London: Marshall, Morgan & Scott, n.d.

Smith, Jacob Brubaker. *A Revelation of Jesus Christ.* Edited by J. O. Yoder. Scottdale, Pa.: Herald, 1961.

Stanton, Gerald B. *Kept From the Hour: Biblical Evidence for the Pretribulational Return of Christ.* Toronto: Evangelical, 1964.

Swete, Henry Barclay. *The Apocalypse of St. John.* 2nd ed. London: Macmillan, 1907.

————., ed. *The Old Testament in Greek According to the Septuagint.* Vols. 1-3. Cambridge: Cambridge U., 1887.

Tenney, Merrill C. *Interpreting Revelation.* Grand Rapids: Eerdmans, 1957.

Thiessen, Henry Clarence. *Introduction to the New Testament.* Grand Rapids: Eerdmans, 1943.

————. *Introductory Lectures in Systematic Theology.* Grand Rapids: Eerdmans, 1956.

Thompson, Frank C. *The New Chain-Reference Bible.* 3rd ed. Indianapolis: Kirkbride, 1957.

Torrance, Thomas F. *The Apocalypse Today.* Grand Rapids: Eerdmans, 1959.

Walvoord, John F. *The Rapture Question.* Findlay, O.: Dunham, 1957.

————. *The Revelation of Jesus Christ.* Chicago: Moody, 1966.

Williams, H. C. *The Revelation of Jesus Christ.* Cincinnati: Standard, 1917.

Young, Robert. *Analytical Concordance to the Bible.* 22nd American ed. Grand Rapids: Eerdmans, 1955.

Other Sources

Abernathy, William E., "The Seventy Weeks of Daniel 9:24-27." Master's dissertation, Faith Theological Seminary, 1958.

Beasley-Murray, G. R. "Revelation." In *The New Bible Commentary*, 2nd ed., edited by F. Davidson, pp. 1168-1199. Grand Rapids: Eerdmans, 1958.

Binkley, H. Keith. "Meaning of the Seven Heads in Revelation 17:9." B.D. critical monograph, Grace Theological Seminary, 1959.

Burke, John P. "The Identity of the Twenty-Four Elders of Revelation 4:4." B.D. critical monograph, Grace Theological Seminary, 1959.

Cohen, Gary G. "The Chronology of the Book of Revelation." Th.D. dissertation, Grace Theological Seminary, 1966.

————. "Hermeneutical Principles and Creation Theories," *Grace Journal*, vol. 5, no. 3 (fall 1964), pp. 17-23.

Cooper, David L. *The Antichrist and the World-Wide Revival: A Study of II Thessalonians 2:1-12*. Los Angeles: Biblical Research Society, 1954.

————. *The Invading Forces of Russia and of the Antichrist Overthrown in Palestine (Ezekiel 38-39)*. Los Angeles: Biblical Research Society, n.d.

————. *Will the Church Go Through the Tribulation? (Luke 21)."* Los Angeles: Biblical Research Society, n.d.

Hodges, Zane C. "The First Horseman of the Apocalypse." *Bibliotheca Sacra*, vol. 119, no. 476 (Oct.-Dec. 1961), pp. 324-34.

Hoyt, Herman A. "Apocalypse." Mimeographed syllabus. Winona Lake, Ind.: Grace Theological Seminary, n.d.

Julien, Thomas T. "The War in Heaven—Revelation 12:7-9." B.D. critical monograph, Grace Theological Seminary, 1957.

Kent, Homer A., Jr. "Matthew." In *The Wycliffe Bible Commentary*, edited by Charles F. Pfeiffer and Everett F. Harrison, pp. 929-85. Chicago: Moody, 1962.

Orr, James. "Revelation of John." In *The International Standard Bible Encyclopaedia*, vol. 4, pp. 2582-2587. Grand Rapids: Eerdmans, 1957.

Rich, Norville J., Sr. "The Meaning of the Phrase, 'On the Lord's Day' in Revelation 1:10." B.D. critical monograph, Grace Theological Seminary, 1947.

Rissi, Mathias. "The Rider on the White Horse," *Interpretation: A Journal of Bible and Theology*, vol. 18, no. 4 (Oct. 1964), pp. 407-18.

Shattuck, Grant Duane. "A Critical Investigation of Revelation 17:5." B.D. critical monograph, Grace Theological Seminary, 1956.

Smith, Wilbur M. "Revelation." In *The Wycliffe Bible Commentary*, *edited by Charles F. Pfeiffer and Everett F. Harrison*, pp. 1491-1525. Chicago: Moody, 1962.

Smouse, Glenn Ellsworth. "The Church in the Olivet Discourse." Master's dissertation, Grace Theological Seminary, 1962.

Whitcomb, John C., Jr. "Daniel's Great Seventy-Week Prophecy: An Exegetical Insight," pp. 1-4. (Paper delivered at the Seventh Foreign Language Conference of the University of Kentucky, Lexington, Ky., April 23, 1954.)

Zahn, Theodor. "The Writings of John." In *Introduction to the New Testament*, translated by M. W. Jacobus et al., 3:174-449. Edinburgh: T. & T. Clark, 1909.